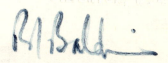

Revision Notes
on
Building Services

N. Davison. M.I.O.B., A.R.S.H.

and

H. Taylor. B. Arch., R.I.B.A.

Department of Surveying and Construction,
Newcastle upon Tyne Polytechnic

LONDON

NEWNES-BUTTERWORTHS

CONTENTS

INTRODUCTION

This book is not intended to be a formal textbook. It has been designed to identify and set out in a readily assimilated form the main points and basic facts which a student would expect to relate to each of the topics generally covered by a Building Services syllabus. Arranged in a 'notebook' form, the pages which refer to each of the subject items can be used either as initial lecture notes (to be enlarged upon by further study) or as a set of revision notes. As such, certain trigger words and points are therefore emphasised.

To produce a satisfactory environment a building must contain, or be served by, additional items which increase its convenience and efficiency. Many of these items are grouped under a general heading of Building Services and the scope, complexity and value of the design, use and installation of these specialised services within the Building Industry are increasing rapidly.

Basically, the services can be grouped as follows: services which can be said to contribute to a more convenient use of the building in the form of artificial lighting, heating, ventilation and air conditioning; services which contribute to the more efficient running of the building as an environmental unit, such as sanitation, drainage and water supply installations; services which can materially assist the user of the building, such as lifts, escalators and refuse disposal systems.

The first group, while being considered necessary in a building need not be interdependent. The second group however, which can almost be described as essential includes services which are interrelated and dependent on each other. The third group can almost be classed as optional depending on the degree or otherwise of the convenience desired.

With these three groups in mind, this book is arranged so that a complete page deals with a complete subject or an individual part of a subject which can follow on or be introductory to other parts of the section.

Today, Building Services have become increasingly important and can account for 50 % of the initial cost of the building in some cases, and for 80% of the running cost of the building.

As the demands of the users of buildings increase, so the 'Services Machinery, contained within the envelope of the building will expand. Therefore, a clear understanding of the basics of Building Services is all important.

The authors would like to express their thanks to Norma Lupton for her help in the preparation of the illustrations.

Sources of information are acknowledged as follows:

BIBLIOGRAPHY AND REFERENCES

It is suggested, in conjunction with the revision notes, that this list forms the basis for further reading and study, as may be required.

British Standards, British Standards Institution.
British Standard Codes of Practice, British Standards Institution.
The Building Regulations, H.M.S.O.
Regulations for the Electrical Equipment of Buildings, Inst. Elect. Engrs.
Building Research Establishment Digests, H.M.S.O.
D. of E. Advisory Leaflets, H.M.S.O.
Electrics 72/73, The Electricity Council.
Architects Journal Handbook, Building Services.
Specification, Architectural Press.

Woolley,L. *Drainage Details in SI Metric,* Northwood Publications.
Blake,E.H. *Drainage and Sanitation,* Batsford.
Burberry, P. *Environment and Services,* Batsford.
Faber, O. and Kell, J.R. *Heating and Air Conditioning of Buildings,* Architectural Press.
Institution of Heating and Ventilating Engineers Guide.

Manufacturing catalogues of specialist firms.

SOURCE OF SUPPLY

    (a) Surface springs - variable supply - possible pollution.
    (b) Bore holes - shallow - deep - artesian.
    (c) Rivers or streams - invariably polluted - requiring full treatment.
    (d) Lakes and reservoirs - also polluted and requiring full treatment.
    (e) Rainwater direct - paved areas formed for catchment.

QUALITY

Examination of source of origin and complete chemical and bacteriological examination will determine this. Colour, odour and taste also regarded as important with Water Authorities today.

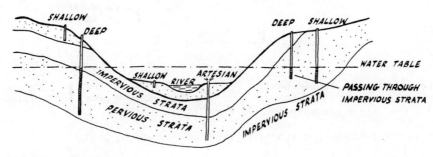

TYPES OF BOREHOLE

TREATMENT Determined by quality -

    (a) Screening - removal of large particles.
    (b) Sedimentation - chemically assisted by use of alum, forming coagulant.
    (c) Filtration - removal of small particles - mechanical and biological

      (i) Slow sand.
     (ii) Rapid gravity.
    (iii) Pressure type.

    (d) Sterilisation - chlorination most common - 0.2 parts per million.
    (e) Aeration - cascade, spray or injection type - increases oxygen content - gives sparkle.
    (f) Fluoridation - calcium fluoride added - 1 part per million - helps to prevent tooth decay.

TESTING

Tests require expert interpretation with regard to pollution, solids, salts, degree of hardness (temporary and permanent) metals, bacteria, viruses.

MAINS DISTRIBUTION

(a) Water Board: *Domestic* - Fully treated.
(b) Water Board: *Industrial* - Partially treated
                           Usually chlorinated.
(c) Large industrial complexes may provide and treat their
    own supply.

Service reservoir. Sited to give ideal range of static head where possible.

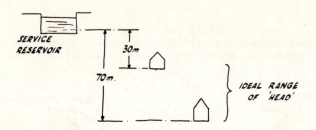

Basic pressure created by 30m head 300 kN/m^2 approx
Basic pressure created by 70m head 700 kN/m^2 approx   STATIC HEAD
(1m head gives static pressure of 9.81 kN/m^2)

ACTUAL DRAW OFF PRESSURE AND FLOW will fluctuate depending on:

(a) Hydraulic gradient.
(b) Demand at any specific time.
(c) Point of connection.

WATER MAINS

Materials: Cast iron, steel, asbestos cement, unplasticised P.V.C.
Location: Under carriageway most common (coordination of services
          recommended in recent years but this is not often implemented).
Layout: A grid pattern from two or more trunk mains giving in effect
          a *ring* service to any position.

Tapping of mains under pressure

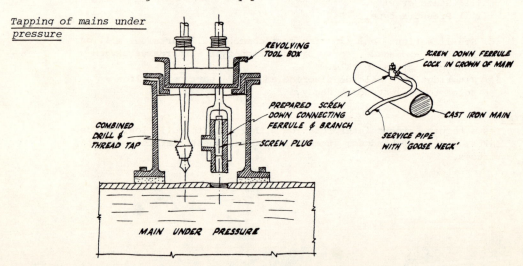

GENERAL DISTRIBUTION

Communication pipe: Responsibility of supply authority, running from main
to stop cock, just _outside_ curtilage. Right angles to main for easy
location. Connection in direction of main with 'gooseneck' to allow
for differential movement. Minimum depth: 0.75m.

Service pipe: Stop cock to fitment - under _mains_ pressure. Minimum joints
below ground.

Distribution pipes: Storage tank to fitments - under _tank_ pressure.

Protection against frost: Pipe runs taken up inside walls wherever possible.
Lag all pipes and tanks in roof space and pipes below ground floor level.

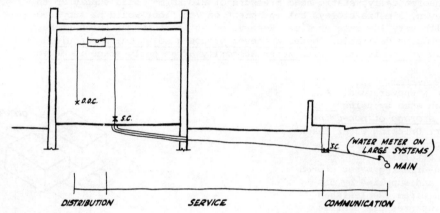

DISTRIBUTION SYSTEMS (Note. Refer to Local Authority before selecting type of system).

(A) Direct system

Common in Northern England where
all cold water is generally drawn
direct from main (except possibly
high rise development)

(B) Indirect system

More common in Southern England. Drinking
water and storage system only supplied
direct from main. Water authority may have
statutory power to insist on this. Enables
bulk of water to be stored at non peak periods.

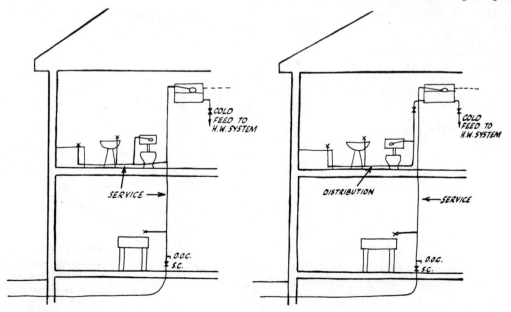

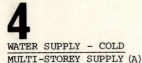

SUPPLY TO MULTI-STOREY BUILDINGS - GENERAL

Basic requirements: *Economic* to install and operate.
Adequate flow rate provided
Continuous supply.
Suitable *working pressure*

<u>Static pressure</u> 1m head gives static pressure of 9.81 kN/m^2 (approx.10 kN/m^2)
3m head (1 normal storey) gives approx. 30 kN/m^2.

<u>Variation in mains pressure</u>. Due to variations in hydraulic gradient, pipe
sizing, valving, demand and general flow patterns.

<u>Static head available in mains</u>. Ideal between 30 and 70 metres.

<u>Static head desirable in buildings</u>. (30 to 45 metres) (10 to 15 storeys)
Theoretically, static head pressure of 210 kN/m^2 would supply up to
seven, 3 metre storeys but equipment on 7th floor would be supplied
with very low rate of flow. Reserve of at least two or three storeys
would be desirable. (Note. Whatever proposed solution, it should
always be discussed with Water Authority at an early stage in design.)

UNBOOSTED SUPPLY

Desirable whenever possible.
May be achieved by using *ring
main and storage of non-drinking water*. Drinking water taken
direct from ring service pipe
- demand determines flow pattern. Non-drinking water stored
in tanks and supplied by distribution pipes. Replenished
under mains pressure over 24
hour period through ball valves.

Storage tanks
One day supply. Access <u>cover</u>
supplied. <u>Overflow</u> must be
correctly sized. Tank 'married'
correctly to avoid stagnation.
Provision of 'safe' should always be considered. Guard
against frost.

<u>Diagram</u> shows non-boosted
supply with mains pressure of
approx. 250 kN/m^2. This would
take water up six storeys with
some in reserve.

All distribution pipes are
NOT shown.

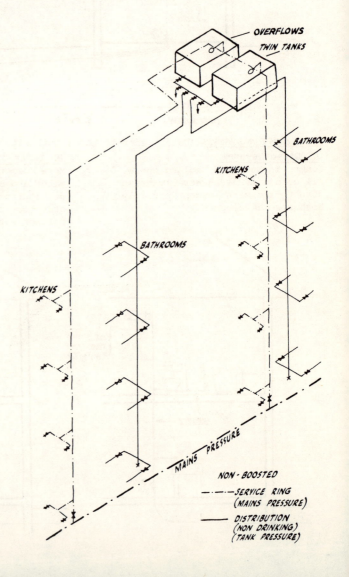

OVERFLOWS

TWIN TANKS

BATHROOMS

KITCHENS

BATHROOMS

KITCHENS

MAINS PRESSURE

NON-BOOSTED

—·—·—·— SERVICE RING
(MAINS PRESSURE)

——————— DISTRIBUTION
(NON DRINKING)
(TANK PRESSURE)

BOOSTED SUPPLY

Method used depends on *local circumstances*, *water authority* and *cost*.

Pumping 1. *Direct* from main unsatisfactory - possible back siphonage and back pressure which could fracture main (extreme).

2. *Indirect* with break tank between mains and pump. Break tank relatively small to ensure quick turnover so no stagnation. *Special* construction for *drinking* water.

Pump control

(a) Water level control
(b) Water pressure control

(a) Water level control

1 High level storage necessary
2 Main control by float switches
3 Duplicate pumps - valves/non-return valves
4 Drinking water points above mains pressure level supplied by storage header (alternative separate storage tank at roof level)
5 Pipe line switch (water level control) on time delay unit controlling pumps to replenish drinking water.

   Refer Pullen Pumps Ltd for pump details - pages 5 and 6.

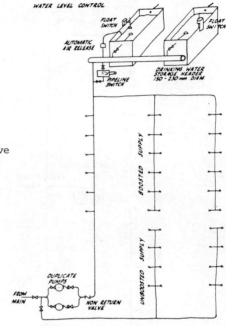

(b) Water pressure control

1 High level storage not necessary.
2 Artificial pressure by pressure vessel
3 All equipment in pump room
4 Pump controlled by pressure switch
5 Air replenished by compressor controlled by float switch
6 Ball valves to storage tanks delay action type to conserve pressure and pumping.

N.B. In both cases non-boosted supply to be direct from main and taken as high as practicable.

Drinking water storage tank to have fitted dust tight *cover*, full *access*, *locked vent* and *overflow* with *mesh filter* , correct overflow *size* and *sample* cock.

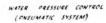

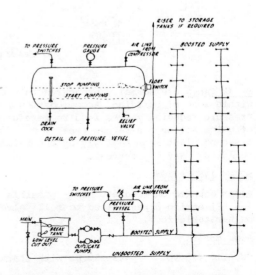

6

WATER SUPPLY - COLD
MULTI-STOREY SUPPLY (C)

BUILDINGS OVER 15 STOREYS

As building increases in height, then *storage of cold water at roof level* puts added
weight on structure. Bulk storage could take place at low level with supplementary
storage tanks installed at 10 or 15 storey levels to give *reasonable static pressure*
in downward distribution pipes.

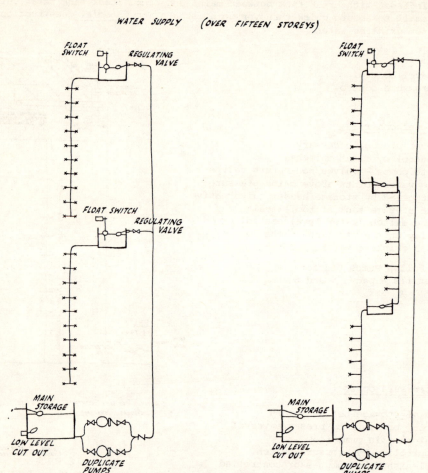

WATER SUPPLY   (OVER FIFTEEN STOREYS)

ALTERNATIVE ARRANGEMENTS.

Break tanks are normally preferred to pressure reducing valves in limiting pressure
within zone of building. Accommodation required for tank - foolproof.
Pressure reducing valves require careful maintenance. Non-return valves should be
of quick acting non-return type.
A second plant room half way up the building should be considered for very high
buildings (say 100 metres).

SOUND INSULATION

Pumps mounted on concrete bed - possible cork sandwich used. Water velocities kept
low. Silencing pipes fitted to ball valves. Careful siting of pumps - not bordering
on habitable room.

N.B.

Pump motors

Usually 415 volt 3-phase 50 Hz with starter.

DOMESTIC HOT WATER

Direct - for small dwellings - domestic water only. Possible problems. Consider
temporary hardness in _primary circulation_ and furring up.

Indirect - water as heating medium and usable hot water separated. Heating by
calorifier or indirect cylinder. Two feed and expansion tanks technically
better (no mixing, less corrosion).

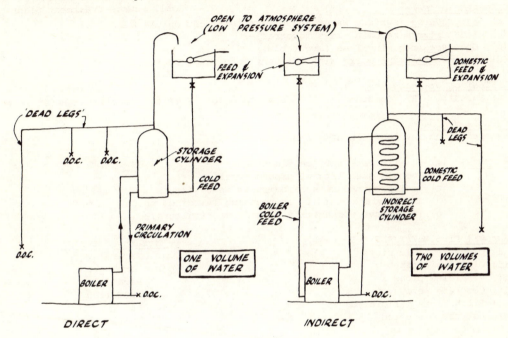

Dead legs - No circulation, water cools and so possible wastage running off. Acceptable length of dead legs (Water Byelaws) pipe diam - length e.g. up to
18 mm ∅ (12 m), 18 mm - 25 mm (8 m), over 25 mm (3 m).

Secondary circulation - provides hot water circulation gravity or accelerated.
Suitable for HIGH RISE building - avoiding too long dead legs.
Note: Primary flow and return may be low pressure hot water, high pressure
hot water or steam.

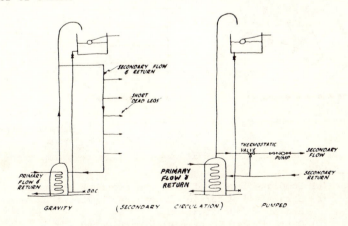

8

DRAINAGE - GENERAL AND SUBSOIL and
SYSTEMS INTRODUCTION

DRAINAGE BELOW GROUND   Drain: That within curtilage of building (except 'private sewer')

TYPE of drain	_DISCHARGE of drain_
(a) Subsoil	(a) Combined sewer
(b) Surface water	(b) Surface water sewer
(c) Foul water	(c) Foul water sewer
(d) Combined (foul and surface)	(d) Soakaway (surface water or effluent)
	(e) Cesspool (foul water only)
	(f) Small sewage treatment plant

DISCHARGE of Sewer

(a) _Watercourse_ (surface water and treated effluent only) - N.B.
(b) Tidal _river_ (becoming less favourable)
(c) Open _sea_ (becoming less favourable)
(d) Sewage _treatment works_ with effluent into water course.

SYSTEMS of drainage

(A) Subsoil   (B) Combined   (C) Separate   (D) Partially separate (Refer Sheet No 9)

Subsoil drainage
Exempted from any requirements of B.Reg. part N.

Purpose: (a) To eliminate surface flooding
             (b) Improve stability of ground surface
             (c) To lessen the risk if dampness in basements
             (d) To alleviate humidity surrounding buildings on damp sites
             (e) To improve workability of soil (agricultural)

Subsoil Pipe MATERIALS	_Pattern of LAYING_
(i) Clayware field pipes	(a) Natural
(ii) Clay drain pipes	(b) Herringbone
(iii) Vitrified pipes	(c) Parallel
(iv) Concrete porous	(d) Grid iron
(v) Pitch fibre perforated	(e) Fan
(vi) Polythene slotted	(f) Moat or cut off

(a) FOLLOW NATURAL CONTOURS

(c) ONE SIDED HERRINGBONE (PARALLEL)

(e) CONVERGING (FAN)

(b) HERRINGBONE

(d) GRID IRON

(f) MOAT

SUBSOIL DRAINAGE

Choice of system depends on site conditions but it is very important that _an efficient outfall be provided_.

Design factors   (a) Complete levels of site and contours plotted.
                   (b) Strata and water level obtained by trial holes
                       and site investigation.
                   (c) Outfall must be carefully considered.

SYSTEM A. Refer to sub-soil drains; Sheet no. 8.

System B. Combined system

Combined drain and sewer takes _both_
foul and surface water.
Very popular in the past.
Simplest and usually cheapest layout.
No chance of connecting to wrong drain.
House drains well flushed with S.W.
Storm overflows may be necessary but
may lead to river pollution.
Possible silting in dry weather.
If pumping required it means pumping
foul and surface water.
Could cause difficulties with sewage
treatment works.
Suitable if discharging into open
sea, with purification by dilution.

System C. Separate system

Separate drains and sewers for
foul and _surface_ water.
Soakaways may be used for surface
water. The trend today.
Foul water treated - S.W. to water
course.
Pipes usually cross each other -
costly.
More pre-planning required with
regard to levels.
Risk of connecting to wrong drain.
No need for storm overflows.
Small flows may require flushing
of foul water drain.
Pumping may only be required for
foul water.
Foul water only - relieves sewage
treatment works.

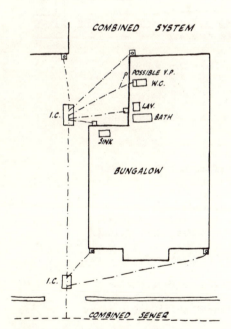

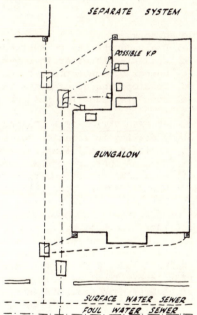

System D. Partially separate system

As name suggests, a compromise between combined and separate.
Gives a certain amount of relief to treatment works.

FACTORS GOVERNING CHOICE OF SYSTEM

  (i) Local authority requirements
     (by far the most important).
 (ii) Relative cost.
(iii) Possibility of pumping required.
 (iv) Outfall availability.

  (v) Gradient availability.
 (vi) Distance to sewer, stream
     or treatment works.
(vii) Present and future sewer
     availability.

General aim

To provide system of self cleansing pipework by which foul and surface
water may be speedily and efficiently conveyed, without risk of nuisance
or danger to health.

10

DRAINAGE

PRIVATE SEWER and PREPARATION OF DRAINAGE SCHEME

THE PRIVATE SEWER

Drains from each property are connected to a common 'drain' termed a
'private sewer'. One connection is then made to the public sewer.
Combined or separate systems. Only with Local Authority approval.
Most Local Authorities accept the 'private sewer'in principle.

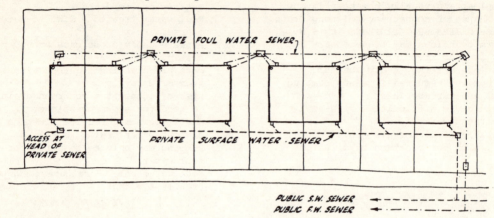

PUBLIC S.W. SEWER
PUBLIC F.W. SEWER

Possible advantages

    (a) Drain depths may be kept comparatively shallow throughout.
    (b) Total length of drain may be reduced.
    (c) Number of connections to main public sewer reduced.
    (d) Less opening up of roads required.
    (e) Possible reduction in number of inspection chambers required

NOTES ON THE PREPARATION OF A DRAINAGE SCHEME:

  (a) Study drawing in relation to:
     (i) Position of all sanitary equipment and surface water catchment.
    (ii) General contours of land and direction of fall.
   (iii) Possible outfall position for foul and surface water.
    (iv) Whether separate or combined system is required.
     (v) Level of outfall position - is it going to be 'tight' for fall ?
  (b) Plot a workable, economic drain run, keeping branches short (always
     consider alternatives).
  (c) Plot required means of access (inspection chambers and rodding eyes.)
  (d) Give an approx. size for each drain.
  (e) Check on overall fall. (Is entry into sewer going to be tight?)
  (f) Plot invert level of drain inspection chambers (accurately) starting
     at head of main drain if entry into sewer is'easy' or at sewer entry
     if entry into sewer is'tight'.
  (g) Re-check system for any better alternative arrangement.
  (h) Compile inspection chamber schedule.

  Note: In practice when large installations are being designed, then all
      possible alternatives should be considered from the point of
      view of efficiency and of course economy (capital cost and main-
      tenance costs).

THE KEY TO ANY DRAINAGE SYSTEM IS SIMPLICITY

PRINCIPLES

Foul water: Discharge from sink, lavatory, W.C.,bidet, bath and shower
(all discharge other than rainwater).

Surface water: Unpolluted rainwater only.

Principles and rules (refer to Building Regulations Part N)

(a) Suitable sound materials of adequate strength.

(b) Laid to falls to give self cleansing gradient (unless pumped or ejected).

(c) Laid in *straight line* between change of gradient or direction.

(d) Drains to be *durable* regarding the matter passing through them and the ground through which the drain may pass. (Protection against corrosion etc.)

(e) All *joints* must be of appropriate material - *watertight* under movement and form no obstruction inside pipes.

(f) *Minimum* internal diameter - (foul drains 100 mm) (S.W. 75 mm) Never less than pipes, appliance or drain which it serves or which pass into it.

(g) Drain passing under building should be adequately supported and be accessible throughout its length for cleaning purposes (e.g. inspection chamber each end).

A drainage system must provide a leakproof, durable, clean and speedy system of disposing of waste water etc. from a building to point of collection or discharge without creating a nuisance.

MATERIALS

1 Rigid pipe-line systems and joints

Must be fully rigid against *all* movement - older traditional method.
Clay socket and spigotted pipes - gaskin and cement mortar joints.
Cast iron socket and spigotted pipes - lead caulked joints.
Concrete socket and spigotted pipes - cement mortar joints.

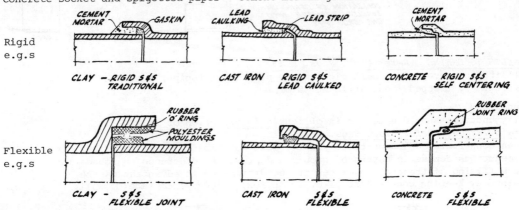

Rigid e.g.s

CLAY — RIGID S&S TRADITIONAL   CAST IRON RIGID S&S LEAD CAULKED   CONCRETE RIGID S&S SELF CENTERING

Flexible e.g.s

CLAY - S&S FLEXIBLE JOINT   CAST IRON S&S FLEXIBLE   CONCRETE S&S FLEXIBLE

2 Flexible pipe-line systems and joints

Modern tendency to use this method wherever possible.
Flexible joint takes up movement and yet remains watertight.
Clay socket and spigotted pipes - rubber gasket O rings - plastic sealing units.
Clay spigotted pipes - polypropylene coupling and rubber sealing rings.
Cast iron socketed and spigotted - bolted glands O rings.
Pitch fibre pipes, tapered ends - sleeve coupling or snap ring jointing.
Concrete socket and spigotted pipes - rubber joint ring.
P.V.C socket and spigotted pipes with - O rings or jointing coupling pieces and rings O type.
Asbestos cement spigotted with sleeve joint - O rings.

12

DRAINAGE
ACCESS, INLET AND TRENCHES

MEANS OF ACCESS - Refer Bldg. Regs. N 12

All parts of drainage systems must be capable of being *inspected* and *cleaned* (by rodding etc.) which requires points of access.

Inspection chamber construction
(a) Sustain load on it.
(b) Watertight.
(c) Adequate size (influenced by size of drain, number of branches and depth).
(d) Non-ventilated cover.
(e) Step irons to provide safe access.
(f) Smooth impervious benching.

Positioning of chamber
(a) At each change of direction or gradient.
(b) 12.5 m from a junction if no access at junction.
(c) At the head of a 'private sewer'.
(d) No point of drain more than 45 m from access.

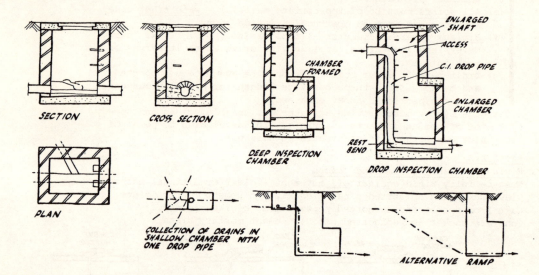

SECTION

CROSS SECTION

DEEP INSPECTION CHAMBER

ENLARGED SHAFT
ACCESS
C.I. DROP PIPE
ENLARGED CHAMBER
CHAMBER FORMED
REST BEND
DROP INSPECTION CHAMBER

PLAN

COLLECTION OF DRAINS IN SHALLOW CHAMBER WITH ONE DROP PIPE

ALTERNATIVE RAMP

INLETS TO DRAINS   Refer Bldg. Regs. N 13

All inlets (except from soil pipe, waste pipe or vent pipe) must be effectively trapped. Seal at least 50 mm.

Junctions

All junctions should enter drain *obliquely in direction of flow*.

Drain TRENCHES Refer Bldg. Regs. N 14

When constructed adjacent to building - must not impair stability of building.
Precautions depend on nature of ground and proximity of trench to foundation.
Back filling of trenches under certain conditions. Most advantage can be
gained by keeping centre line of drain approx. 1.500 m from face of wall.

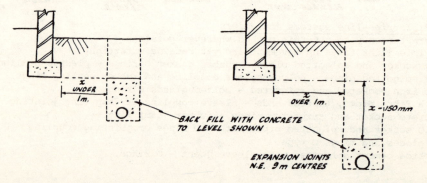

x UNDER 1m.

x OVER 1m.

x - 150mm

BACK FILL WITH CONCRETE TO LEVEL SHOWN

EXPANSION JOINTS N.E. 9m CENTRES

CONNECTION - DRAIN TO SEWER - B. Regs. N 16 (1) (2)

Branch to discharge obliquely into sewer flow. Watertight connection to remain.
Preferably Local Authority work - consider safety - available methods.

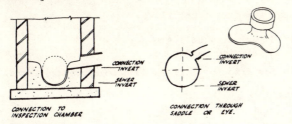

(a) Existing or new I.C.s.
(b) Junction eye or saddle.

N.B. In all cases *check invert levels* to ensure correct falls available.

CONNECTION TO INSPECTION CHAMBER

CONNECTION THROUGH SADDLE OR EYE.

Types of access other than I.C.s

(a) Access pipe or bend (S.W. drain)
(b) Fitting access (gullies, W.C.s)
(c) Rodding eye (used at head of shallow drain)

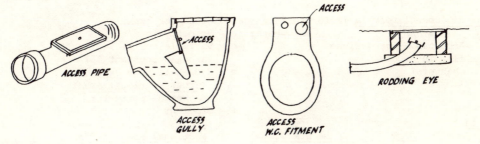

ACCESS PIPE

ACCESS GULLY

ACCESS W.C. FITMENT

RODDING EYE

Ventilation

B. Regs. Part N2, N3, N4 and N7. Ventilating pipe to system. Not a drain, no soil
or S. water. Fresh air terminal at highest point. Avoid NUISANCE.
N.B. Public Health Act 1936 Sect 40 requires soil pipe from W.C. vented. B. Regs
only require vent pipes to prevent break of trap seal.

Sewage lifting By (a) Pumping (substantial flow) or (b) Ejection (smaller infrequent
amounts)

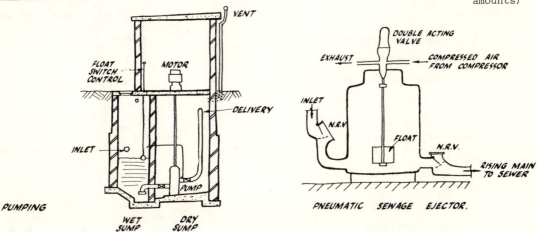

PUMPING

WET SUMP   DRY SUMP

PNEUMATIC SEWAGE EJECTOR.

Avoid if possible maintenance problems - only necessary if drain levels poor or if
sewer likely to surcharge.

DRAINAGE - PIPE SIZING (A)

PIPE SIZING Refer B. Reg. N10 (1)(e) and N10 (2)
Gradient must ensure (unless pumped) self cleansing.
Internal diameter, foul water: 100 mm min.
Internal diameter, surface water: 75 mm min.
C.P. 301 recommends for steady flow - minimum velocity of 0.75 m/s when
flowing 1/4 depth which would give gradient for 100 mm pipe as 1 in 80.

'MAGUIRE'S RULE' Particularly formulated for fractional flows.

$$\left.\begin{array}{lll}
\text{i.e. } 100 \text{ mm} & 1 \text{ in } 40 \\
150 \text{ mm} & 1 \text{ in } 60 \\
225 \text{ mm} & 1 \text{ in } 90
\end{array}\right\} \begin{array}{l}\text{Velocity of 1.4 m/s}\\ \text{flowing half bore.}\end{array}$$

self cleansing when laid to this rule for fractional flows down to approx. ⅛ bore.

Recommended velocities (self cleansing)
Minimum 0.75 m/s to maximum 3 m/s.

Flow velocity influenced by
- (a) Coefficient of friction of pipe surface (not as important as pipe becomes older and lining forms on inside).
- (b) Gravitational unit (9.81).
- (c) Hydraulic mean depth.
- (d) Gradient.

Use of 'Chezy' formula (Refer to later calculation for example)

$$V = c\sqrt{mi}$$

(Acceptable for drainage flow in pipes and channels)

where: V = Velocity in m/s
c = Variable coefficient (often taken as constant 55)
m = Hydraulic mean depth. $\dfrac{(\text{Cross sectional area})}{\text{Wetted perimeter}}$
i = Gradient

Data

Flow	H.M.D. (m)	Sectional area of flow
Full bore	$0.25d$	$0.785d^2$
2/3 bore	$0.291d$	$0.556d^2$
1/2 bore	$0.25d$	$0.393d^2$
1/3 bore	$0.186d$	$0.229d^2$

Discharge from pipes and channels

$$Q = AV$$

where:

Q = Quantity discharged in m³/s

A = Sectional area of *flow* in m²

V = Velocity of flow in m/s

Surface water drains

Typical storm profile.
Intensities last for very short period of time.
Graph shows rate in relation to time together
with frequency.
Intensity of 50mm/hour normally used in
calculations.

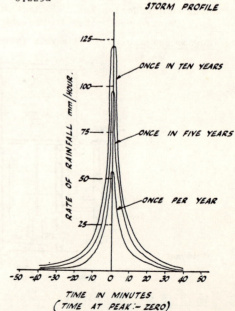

STORM PROFILE

Impermeability factor

Surface	Imp. Factor	
Roofs	0.95	
Roads	0.75 to 0.90	Area may be multiplied
Paths	0.50 to 0.75	by its respective factor
Gardens	0.10	

Design of surface water drain (Example)

Data: Area of run off 2000 m²
Impermeability factor 0.90
Rainfall intensity 50 mm/hour
Reasonable assumptions - Velocity 1 m/s at one third bore.

$$\text{Run off} = \frac{\text{Area x mm/hr x I.F.}}{1000 \text{ x } 3600} \text{ (m}^3\text{/s)} = \frac{2000 \text{ x } 50 \text{ x } 0.9}{3600 \text{ x } 1000} = \underline{0.025 \text{ m}^3\text{/s}}$$

$$Q = AV$$
$$A = 0.025 \div 1 \text{ m}^2$$
$$0.229d^2 = 0.025$$

$$d = \sqrt{\frac{0.025}{0.229}} = \sqrt{0.109} = \underline{0.330 \text{ m}} \text{ (reasonable practical size would be}$$
$$300 \text{ mm)}.$$

Fall of drain

Example
use of
Chezy
formula

$$V = c\sqrt{mi}$$

$$i = \frac{V^2}{C^2 m} = \frac{1^2}{55^2 \text{ x } 0.186 \text{ x } 0.300}$$

$$= \frac{1}{168.8} \qquad \text{Therefore fall} = \underline{1 \text{ in } 169}$$

Foul water drains

Several unknown factors - assumptions must be made.
Factors to be considered:

    (a) Water consumption per head (suggested 225 litres/head/day)
    (b) Population (up to 4.5 per house)
    (c) Variations in flow (average over 6 hour period approx. 112 litres)
    (d) Peak discharges (4 to 6 times average)
    (e) Possible trade waste
    (f) Possible surface water.

$$\text{Flow} = \frac{\frac{1}{2} \text{ consumption in litres/head/day x population x (4 to 6)}}{6 \text{ hours x } 3600}$$

      (expressed in litres/second)

Example: Data

      20 houses
    225 litres/head/day
     4 persons per house

$$\text{Average rate of flow} = \frac{225 \text{ x } 20 \text{ x } 4}{2 \text{ x } 6 \text{ x } 3600}$$

$$= \underline{0.42 \text{ litres/second}}$$

$$\text{Maximum rate of flow} = 6 \text{ x average}$$
$$= 6 \text{ x } 0.42$$
$$= 2.52 \text{ litres/second}$$
$$\text{or} = \underline{0.0025 \text{ m}^3\text{/s}}$$

DRAINAGE - SEWAGE DISPOSAL

SEWAGE DISPOSAL
Small domestic sewage treatment works
Ref. C.P. 302.100   B. Regs. Part N 17

Small disposal system where unstable organic matter is converted to a stable
inactive matter with effluent taken to a stream or soakaway.

Principle
(a) *Anaerobic* bacteria break down solids in *enclosed* chamber.
(b) *Aerobic* bacteria purify liquid passing through *open* filter.

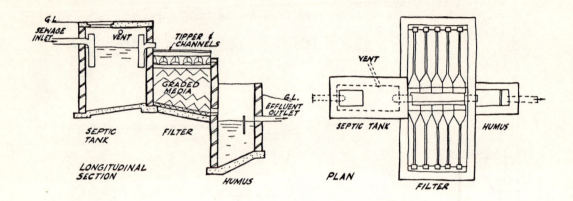

SEPTIC TANK

B. Reg. require minimum 2.7 m³
Plan shape in ratio of 3:1 (more even flow)
Submerged inlets and outlets (less turbulence)
Single tank or two tanks in series.
Effective capacity $C = 140N + 1820$ litres
(where N = number of residents in full time residence which
is halved for part time residence).
Adequately ventilated.

Filter   Biological and mechanical.
Open to atmosphere and amply ventilated at base.
Effluent distributed *evenly* by means of tipper and perforated
channels.
Hard clinker media - replaceable.
Loading 0.5 to 0.75 m³ per head of population.

Humus tank   Required on larger systems, approx. quarter the size
of septic tank. Used to recover humus.

Location   As far away from habitable building as economically possible.
Minimum of 15 m for works serving up to 10 people, progressive-
ly increased to 100 m for population of 100 or more.
Site above local flood level.
Try to avoid pumping.

Access   Access and made up road (possibly turning space) required
for *heavy* sludge disposal vehicle.

<u>CESSPOOLS</u> Ref CP 302 200 and B. Regs Part N17.
Not to be used if alternatives possible - <u>*impervious*</u> construction essential.

Points of construction

(a) Watertight
(b) Adequate ventilation
(c) No outlet or overflow
(d) Square or round on plan
(e) Adequate and safe access
(f) Max. depth say 5 m.
(g) Intercepting chamber required between cesspool and drain.

CESSPOOLS

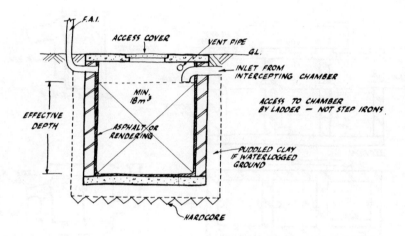

<u>*Capacity*</u> - <u>*Min effective*</u> capacity 18 m³ (B. Regs 1972).

<u>*Points of design*</u> - (foul water basis 120 litres/person/day)

(a) Population involved. (b) <u>*Separate*</u> systems of drainage <u>*necessary*</u>.
(c) Frequency and cost of emptying. (d) Capacity of emptying vehicle.
(e) Access to site of cesspool.

<u>*Points of location*</u> - (Future connection of drainage system to public sewer?)

(a) Preferably sloping site away from building.
(b) Avoidance of nuisance and contamination to buildings and
     water supplies.

<u>*Testing*</u>

Watertight - water filled for 48 hours. Fall in water level
to be less than 25 mm.

DRAINAGE - GREASE AND PETROL INTERCEPTION

GREASE AND PETROL INTERCEPTION -Public Health Act 1936 Section 27

Petrol, grease or similar MUST NOT enter drainage system. CP 301 recommends use
of grease traps and petrol interceptors. Type of building and amount of grease
or petrol govern sizes.

Principles - (NB Grease traps or gullies not normal in domestic drainage).

Grease trap - Large surface area so quick cool and solidify of grease.
Deep water seal - (modern use reduced because of detergents)

Petrol interceptors - Deep water seal gully with perforated lifting tray -
Petrol floats to top and is trapped - gully type - private, compartment
type - commercial garages.

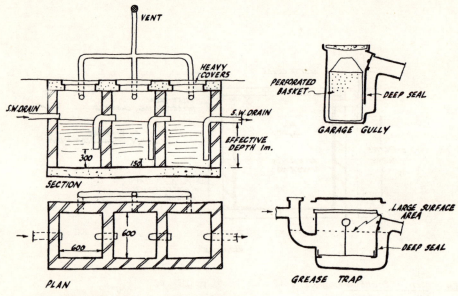

THREE COMPARTMENT PETROL INTERCEPTOR

SOAKAWAYS

Because of tendency to separate drainage systems so possible greater need for
soakaway use. Can be used to dispose final effluent from small sewage works.

Requirements

Adequate storage capacity (large amounts storm water in short period).
Adequate disposal ability (disperse water at average rate of flow in).
Constructed *above water table,* in *permeable strata* and on land lower
than or sloping away from building.

LOCAL AUTHORITIES have powers to test _new_ and _old_ drains and private sewers, under

1. Building Regulations
2. Public Health Act

DIFFERENT AUTHORITIES. Different requirements and _methods_ of testing.

Tests

(a) Watertightness (B. Reg. N11)	Water test
	Air test
	Smoke test
(b) Smoothness of bore	Ball test
(c) Alignment	Lamp and mirror test
(d) Pipe tracing	Colour test
Test must satisfy Local authority	Building Inspector (new work)
	Public Health
	Inspector (old work)

When to test

The Building Regulations state that the test must be carried out after all work and back filling has been completed but it would be advisable to test prior to back filling as well.

In the case of large sewers that can be entered, reliance is often placed on visual inspection of the joints as work proceeds, with an internal examination when completed.

A complete record should always be kept of all tests both during and after construction.

Drain testing equipment

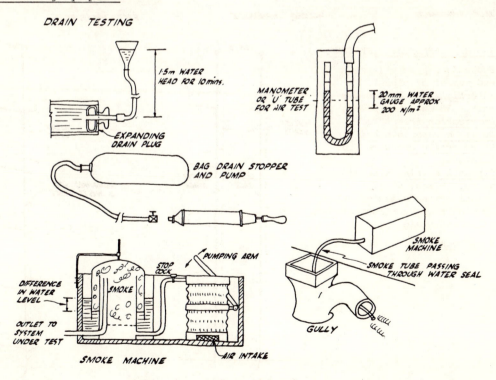

DRAIN TESTING

1.5m WATER HEAD FOR 10mins.

EXPANDING DRAIN PLUG

MANOMETER OR 'U' TUBE FOR AIR TEST

20 mm WATER GAUGE APPROX 200 N/m²

BAG DRAIN STOPPER AND PUMP

SMOKE MACHINE

SMOKE TUBE PASSING THROUGH WATER SEAL

DIFFERENCE IN WATER LEVEL

SMOKE

STOP COCK

PUMPING ARM

OUTLET TO SYSTEM UNDER TEST

AIR INTAKE

SMOKE MACHINE

GULLY

DRAINAGE ABOVE GROUND

Pipe layout and sizes *previously* designed to *rule of thumb* methods.
Subsequent modern design to developments by Building Research Establishment and
American Bureau of Standards.
Building Regulations 1972 Part N3 requires *prevention of destruction of water seal*
in *any trap* in system or in *any appliance* discharging into a system.
Water seal can be destroyed by :

(a) Self syphonage	(d) Evaporation (This can
(b) Induced syphonage } Cause pressure fluctuations	normally be ignored).
(c) Back pressure	

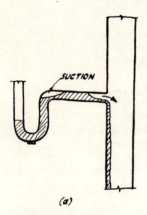

(a)

SELF SIPHONAGE

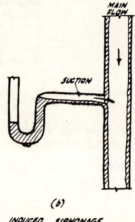

(b)

INDUCED SIPHONAGE

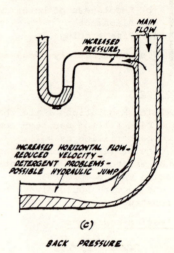

(c)

BACK PRESSURE

GENERAL REQUIREMENTS OF SYSTEMS

(a) *Economic* pipework (size and number of pipes).
(b) *Watertight* (Smoke and air test - 38 mm water/3 mins).
(c) *Obstruction free*
(d) *No air escape* into *building*
(e) *No excessive pressure* fluctuations.
(f) *Pipework within* external walls. (B.Reg. N5 (2))

Full ventilation (classic method of limiting pressure fluctuations) expensive and unsightly.

E.G.s systems (Refer also page 21).

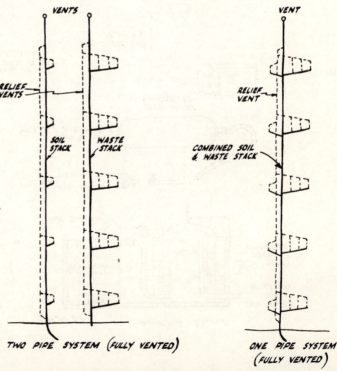

TWO PIPE SYSTEM (FULLY VENTED)

ONE PIPE SYSTEM (FULLY VENTED)

Ventilation for the purpose of *relieving pressure* may be carried out within the soil stack itself. *Full bore* flow *not likely* if sized correctly.

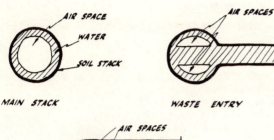

MAIN STACK   WASTE ENTRY

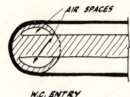

W.C. ENTRY

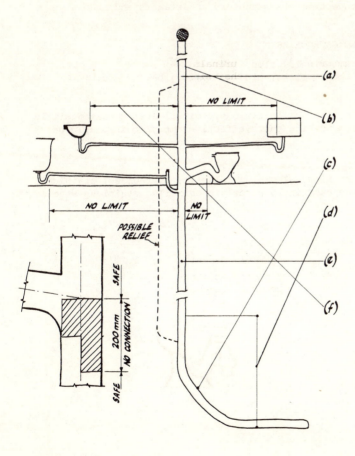

Sketches show *air spaces likely* to occur and act as *ventilation*.

Unvented stacks (single stack system)

Rules to be followed.

(a) Stack must be *straight* (may be offset only above highest branch)
(b) Stack carried up as vent
(c) Connection to drain by easy bend.
(d) Free of connections for a certain distance above drain invert (460 mm, 2 storey) (760 mm tall buildings).
(e) Stack diameter 76-150 mm (to be calculated to prevent overloading)
(f) Branches from lavatory basins not to exceed 1.7 m in length.

Aids to avoiding self and induced syphonage

(i) Deep seal traps.
(ii) Resealing traps.
(iii) Swept W.C. branch connections to stack.
(iv) No bath connection to stack within shaded portion.
(v) Possible use of relief vent (shown dotted on sketch)

Soil stack sizing

Take into consideration maximum anticipated flow. Frequency of use and discharge units for each appliance.

Single stack for office buildings

W.C.s Ranges of *eight* if connected to straight branch. Possible vent required if bends in pipe.

Lav. Basins. Ranges of *four* if connected to straight branch 50mm diameter. Use of spray taps gives a bigger safety margin.
Urinals. Venting *not* normally required - regular cleaning necessary.

*Note:*Refer to B.R.E.Digests 80, 81 and115.Also B.S.C.P. 304.

SANITARY FITMENTS

Accommodation and appliances SPECIFIC or NOT SPECIFIC

1 Laid down by Law - *Specific* and *legally enforceable*

    (a) Factories Act 1961 and accompanying regulations (Sanitary accommodation regulations. Construction Regulations 1966).

    (b) Public Health Acts 1936 and 1961 and amendments.

    (c) Food and Drugs Act 1955 and regulations.

    (d) Offices Shops and Railway Premises Act 1963 and Regulations (San. Convenience Regs 1964) (Washing Facilities Regs 1964)

    (e) The Standard for School Premises Regulations 1959.

    (f) Caravan Sites and Control and Development Act 1960, 1968.

    (g) Agriculture (Safety, Health and Welfare Provision) Act 1956.

2 Laid down by law but *Not Specific.*

    Terms such as 'suitable and sufficient', 'such numbers as may be reasonable'.
    Local authority standards and interpretations of suitable requirements.

3 *Recommended standards*

Refer   (a) Codes of Practice

       (b) Guides by Government departments, stautory undertakers and industry.

Categories

Sanitary fitments grouped in TWO CATEGORIES

    (a) *Soil* fitments - w.c.s, urinals, slop sinks etc.

    (b) *Ablution* fitments - baths, sinks, bidets, lavatory basins etc.

Qualities

    Hard, sound, incorrodible, smooth, impervious, self-cleansing, clean simple attractive design, minimum working parts, effective emptying in simple quick manner.

Materials

    Glazed fireclay, vitreous china, aluminium, plastic, fibreglass, stainless steel. Porcelain enamelled cast iron, porcelain enamelled stainless steel.

SANITARY FITMENTS - TYPES

Washdown w.c. (A)	*Siphonic w.c. (B)*
Gravity overflow discharge principle	Siphonic action contents removal

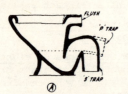

Bidet (C)

Perineal wash. Pop-up waste. Anti contamination provision.

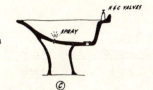

Slab/stall urinal (D)

Automatic flush
4 litres/stall/20 min
8 stalls/outlet.

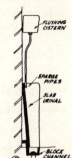

Lavatory basin (F)

(Wash hand basin)
13 mm pillar taps
32 mm waste
Integral overflow
pedestal/bracket.

Bowl urinal (E)

Cheaper -requires responsible use.

Drinking fountain (G)

Fireclay or s.steel part concealed jet hygienic. Trapped outlet.

Belfast sink (H)

Often glazed fireclay. Various sizes. Integral overflow.

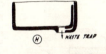

Shower tray (I)

Similar but shallow.

W.C. flushing cistern waste water preventer (J)

Ball valve control.
9-14 litre delivery.

Continuous flushing trough (K)

Low water pressure quick second flush.

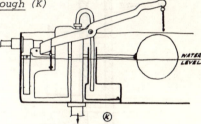

Bath overflow manifold

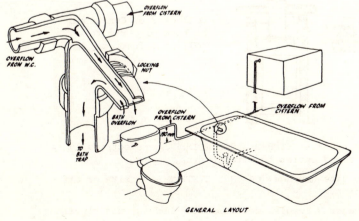

GENERAL LAYOUT

High rise buildings

Common overflow connection to bath. Flush cistern and storage cistern overflow outlets at least 150 mm above bath top edge.

REFUSE DISPOSAL

Ref. CP 306:1972 and BS 1703
   B. Regs. Parts G and J
   B.R.E. Digests. Public Health Act 1936.
B.R.E. estimated domestic refuse yields per dwelling per week (5 persons)

	1968	*1975*	*1980*
Weight (kg)	12.5	14	14
Density (kg/m³)	144	128	120
Volume (m³)	0.085	0.106	0.113

Disposal methods

1 <u>Bins</u> Metal, rubber, plastic - emptying by hand into collecting vehicle. Modern developments of heating systems have added to the problems of disposal.
2 <u>Sacks</u> Paper or plastic - hygienic - higher cost
3 <u>Chute</u> Generally recommended for multi-storey buildings. Refuse preferably wrapped in paper and introduced into chute by means of hopper flaps - self closing.

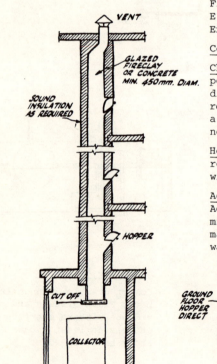

<u>Container chamber</u> Non combustible material. Fire resistance 1 hour or as required of section E 5 B.Regs. Impervious to moisture. Vented. External wall - flush door.

<u>Containers</u> Two per chute. 1.5 to 3 m³ capacity.

<u>Chute</u> As chamber. Vertical if possible but max. permissible offset 60° to horizontal. Min. 450 mm diameter. Sound insulation if next to habitable room (approx 3 brick or 210 mm concrete). If *not* a habitable room (approx ½ brick). Careful planning necessary.

<u>Hoppers</u> Situated in freely vented position. Must remain in *open* or *closed* position. *Not* situated within dwelling. Should be within 30 m of dwelling.

<u>Access</u> Road access provided to collection chambers. Access for inspection and cleaning of chutes after misuse - every third floor. A pintle jet fixture may be incorporated at floor levels for spray washing - drainage then required at base.

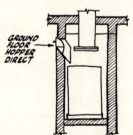

Collector or Container at base of chute to collect refuse.

4 <u>Other systems</u> *Water-borne* to sewer - KITCHEN WASTE GRINDERS - electrically operated - enlarged outlet to kitchen sink.

Water-borne to site storage (GARCHEY SYSTEM) - on site or off site incineration.

Pneumatic conveyor - Swedish development - underground pipelines 0.5 m diameter - high speed delivery to incinerator - high capital cost.

SERVICE DISTRIBUTION SYSTEMS Refer CP413

Modern service requirements have become so vast and complex that they inevitably influence planning and therefore a unified concept of distribution will most likely be settled for at the planning stage.

Group service installations where practicable - *tracing* and *maintenance* simplified.

Environmental problems to be taken into consideration
- (a) *Noise* transmission - air borne and structure borne.
- (b) *Thermal* transmission - possible build up of heat - possible chilling of drinking water.
- (c) *Condensation* - Possible effect on electrical services and thermal insulation.
- (d) *Fire* precautions - Possible compartmentation.

Pattern of distribution
- (a) Service entry duct lead in.
- (b) Main lateral duct.
- (c) Vertical duct.
- (d) Lateral distribution ducts.

VERTICAL distribution invariably requires duct work whereas LATERAL distribution may require duct work, especially to ground floor, but space above suspended ceilings of upper floors may be used to the full (compartmentation against fire must always be considered).

General CATEGORIES of duct:
- (a) Subway - minimum 2 m high walkway.
- (b) Crawlway - mimimum 1 m high.
- (c) Trench - less than 1 m high - access at critical points.
- (d) Vertical - generally internal access.
- (e) Chase (cut recess).
- (f) Casing (enclosure formed on face).

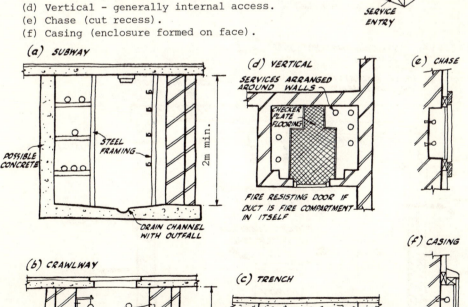

THERMAL ENVIRONMENT

(a) Human thermal comfort.
(b) Environment for process requirements - industry.

It is essential in modern society to produce the _correct environment_ to SUIT
the individual - _not_ the other way around.

Ergonomics. The study of man in relation to his working environment; therefore affecting working conditions.

Problems produced by uncomfortable conditions

(a) Loss of efficiency.
(b) Discontent and indirectly, supply of labour.
(c) Increased sickness.
(d) Increased accident rate.

General aim To achieve environmental conditions whereby comfortable body
temperatures may be maintained by the normal blood flow
variations to the skin.

Basic factors to be taken into consideration

(a) Air temperature   thermometer
(b) Radiant temperature   _measured with_   globe thermometer
(c) Air movement   vane anemometer
(d) Relative humidity   hygrometer

All these factors may only be _collectively_ considered if some form of _air
conditioning_ is installed. In domestic properties, _air temperature_ is often
the only factor really considered and effectively _controlled_.

Whereas _air conditioning_ and the _full control_ of all environmental factors
may be regarded as _desirable_ in all buildings, in certain industrial process
buildings, this control will be regarded as essential.

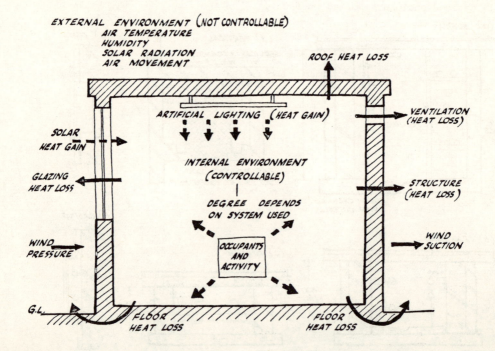

HEAT TRANSMISSION

Definitions and terms	SI unit
Temperature	°C
Temperature interval	deg C
Heat	J (joule)
Calorific value	J/kg
Specific heat capacity	J/kg deg C
Heat flow rate	W (watt)
Density of heat flow rate	W/m²
Conductivity (k value)	W/m deg C
Transmittance	W/m² deg C

Heat transmission coefficients

Note: Terms ending in 'ANCE' designate *overall* properties of a material
and the symbols used are *capital letters*.

Conduct*ance* C. Resist*ance* R. Transmitt*ance* U.

Terms ending in 'IVITY' refer to unit thickness (one metre) of a material
and the symbols used are *lower case* letters.

Conduct*ivity* k. Resist*ivity* r.

Temperature. Degree Celsius (as Centigrade scale) . Freezing 0°C. Boiling 100°C.

Heat.   Considered as any other form of *energy* - joule (J)
Calorific value. Amount of heat energy released when burning a unit mass
            of fuel (J/kg)
Heat flow rate. Used to express heat loss or heat gain *joules per second* (J/s) or
watts. (*Note:* The watt incorporates the basic time factor of the second.)
Density of heat flow rate. Amount of heat (energy) passing through unit
area in unit time (W/m²) .
Thermal conductivity. (k) Amount of *heat energy* conducted through *unit area*
of *unit thickness* with *unit temperature difference* between the two faces.
Watts per square metre of surface area for temperature difference of 1 deg C
per metre thickness.

$$\frac{Wm}{m^2 \ deg \ C} = W/m \ deg \ C$$

Thermal resistivity (r) (reciprocal of conductivity)

$$r = \frac{1}{k}$$

Thermal conductance. This is the surface to surface conductance of a material
or construction and is given as the number of joules per second (watts)
transmitted through 1 m² of the material with 1 deg C difference in *surface*
temperatures.

If *thickness increased* then *conductance reduced*.

$$C = \frac{k}{L} \quad \text{(where } L = \text{thickness in metres)}$$

Thermal resistance. (R) This is resistivity (r) multiplied by thickness (L).

$$R = \frac{L}{k}$$

Specific resistance R_{so} = Outside surface resistance
may be indicated R_{sa} = Resistance of air space
with added suffix R_{si} = Internal surface resistance
thus R_{se} = Earth resistance

Thermal transmittance. (U). Measure of the ability of structure to transmit heat. _Quantity_ of heat that will flow through _unit area_, in _unit time_ per _unit difference_ of temperature between inside and outside environment.

$$U = W/m^2 \text{ deg C}$$

It is the reciprocal of the sum of all the resistances

$$U = \frac{1}{R_{so} + r_{L1} + R_{sa} + r_{L2} + r_{L3} + R_{si}}$$

In calculating U for structure the thermal resistance of each component part must be calculated and the reciprocal of the total R equals U.

$$U = \frac{1}{R \ (total)}$$

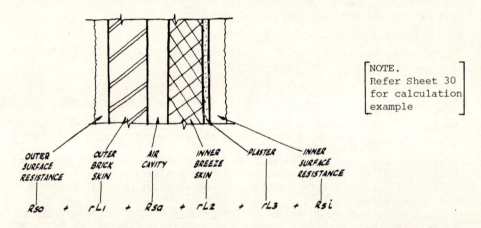

NOTE.
Refer Sheet 30
for calculation
example

Internal surface resistance (R_{si}). This is a variable depending on the direction of heat flow.

Common figure for walls = 0.12 m² deg C/W

External surface resistance (R_{so}). This is a variable depending on element and degree of exposure.

Normal exposure for walls = 0.053 m² deg C/W

Cavity resistance (min. 20 mm) (R_{sa}). This is a variable depending on width of air space, surface emissivity, direction of heat flow and degree of ventilation.

Common figure used = 0.18 m² deg C/W

The following are common conductivity (k) values (W/m degC)

Material	(k)	Material	(k)
Brickwork	1.210	Thermolite	0.202
Dense concrete	1.440	Plasterboard	0.158
Cork slab	0.049	Asbestos cement	0.360
Gypsum plaster	0.461	Glass wool quilt	0.034
Polystyrene	0.033	Wood wool slab	0.093
Softwood	0.138	Cement sand render	0.532
Fibreboard	0.065	Sandstone	1.295

THERMAL INSULATION AND CONSERVATION Ref: D. of E. Housing Development Notes.

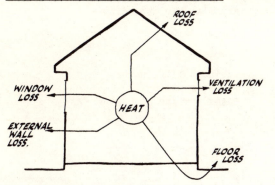

Energy used in U.K.

Space heating	67 %
Water heating	25 %
Lighting	1 %
Other appliances	7 %

Until 31st January 1975, *unit heat losses* were considered for roofs, walls, floors etc. rather than any form of specific heat loss from a particular room. This therefore did *not* take into account *window sizes* in relation to the overall loss.

New mandatory requirements for *new* dwellings - enforceable from 31st January 1975. Ref: The Building Regulations (Second Amendment) 1974.

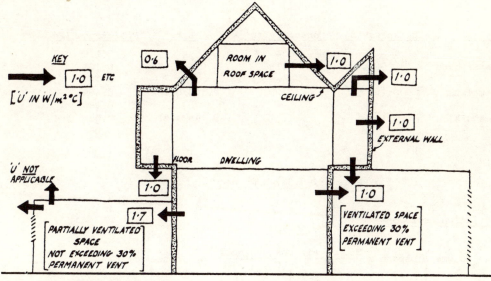

Note: The calculated average *U* value of perimeter walling (including any opening therein) shall not exceed 1.8 W/m² deg C.

Application of higher thermal insulation standards to traditional construction

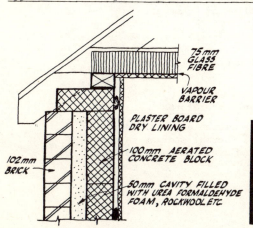

Other points of improvement

(a) *Weatherstripping* reduces draughts giving greater comfort. Increases sound insulation.

(b) *Double glazing* reduces cold air flows near glass - helps overcome condensation problems.

(c) Radical redesign of external envelope is taking place - great emphasis must be placed on vapour barriers.

Note: The present trend is towards *higher heating standards*, therefore greater energy demands.

Older people need higher temperature for comfortable living and there will be more older people by the year 2000.

There is therefore a strong case for *these and even higher levels of thermal insulation* for dwellings to make more efficient use of energy.

CALCULATING 'U' VALUES FROM 'k' VALUES OF MATERIALS

'k' (Conductivity) value for most materials may vary slightly depending
on porosity, moisture content etc.

Example

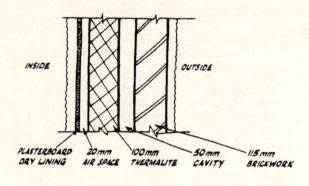

Cavity wall structure
with dry lining.
normal degree of exposure.

PLASTERBOARD DRY LINING — 20mm AIR SPACE — 100mm THERMALITE — 50mm CAVITY — 115mm BRICKWORK

Material	Thickness 'L'	Conductivity 'k'	L/k	Resistance 'R'
R_{si}	–	–	–	0.120
Plasterboard	0.016	0.158	0.016/0.158	0.101
R_{sa}	–	–	–	0.180
Thermalite	0.100	0.202	0.100/0.202	0.495
R_{sa}	–	–	–	0.180
Brickwork	0.115	1.210	0.115/1.210	0.095
R_{so}	–	–	–	0.053

Total R = 1.224

$$U = \frac{1}{R} = \frac{1}{1.224} = \underline{0.817} \text{ W/m}^2 \text{ degC}$$

Ventilation heat loss

$$= \text{Volume of space } \times \frac{\text{No. of air changes/hour}}{3600} \times \text{Volumetric S.H.} \times \text{Temp. Diff.}$$

(m^3) (No. of air changes/sec)   (1300 J/m³ degC)   (degC)

$$\frac{1300}{3600} = \underline{0.36} \quad \text{(Coefficient used in following example)}.$$

Ventilation rates

This may be calculated in m³/s when density of occupation is known or
given as number of air changes per hour, which will vary with type of
building and use of room.

Internal design temperatures		*External design temperatures*
Living and dining rooms	21°C	Influenced by - degree of exposure,
Bedrooms	16°C	pattern of use, thermal storage capacity
Offices	20°C	of structure and overload capacity of
Classrooms	18°C	plant. (-1°C to -3°C)

(These figures are arbitrary)

EXAMPLE IN CALCULATION OF HEAT LOSSES

Sun lounge

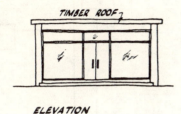

ELEVATION

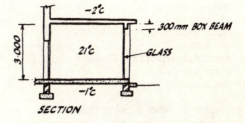

SECTION

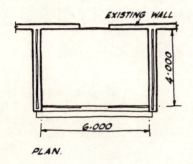

PLAN.

DATA:-

CONCRETE FLOOR	'U' = 2.45 w/m² deg. C
TIMBER ROOF	'U' = 1.25 w/m² deg. C
GLASS	'U' = 4.68 w/m² deg. C
BOX BEAM	'U' = 1.82 w/m² deg. C
BRICKWORK	'U' = 1.70 w/m² deg. C

DESIGN TEMP = 21°C   OUTSIDE TEMP = -2°C

ADJ. ROOM TEMP = 21°C   UNDERFLOOR TEMP = -1°C

AIR CHANGES 2/HOUR   - COEFFICIENT 0.36

Construction	Vol/Area	A/C	U	Temp. Diff. (degC)	Watts
Ventilation	72 m³	2	0.36	23	1192
Cavity walls	24 m²	–	1.70	23	938
Glass	16.2 m²	–	4.68	23	1744
Floor	24 m²	–	2.45	22	1294
Roof	24 m²	–	1.25	23	690
Box beam	1.8 m²	–	1.82	23	75
Exist. wall & door	(no heat losses)			Nil	–
					5933

(Vol/area x (A/C) x (U) x (Temp. Diff. (deg C)) = Watts   Approx. 6 kW

Modification of 'U' value (due to variations in construction)

(a) Calculate the reciprocal of the *U* value. This gives the total resistance of the construction including surface resistances and air spaces.

(b) *Deduct* the Resistance (*R*) of any layer that is to be omitted.

(c) *Add* the Resistance (*R*) of any layer that is to be added.

(d) Calculate the reciprocal of the figures resulting from stage (c) to obtain the new *U* value.

LOW PRESSURE HOT WATER SYSTEMS

(Systems under atmospheric pressure)

Basic essentials

- (A) Water heater
- (B) Expansion tank (feed tank)
- (C) Open vent
- (D) Cold feed
- (E) Heat transmitting element
- (F) Flow pipe
- (R) Return pipe

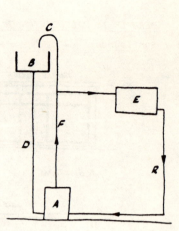

(1) Gravity system   Where the flow of water relies entirely on the difference in densities and static head of the flow and return water.

Motive force exerted = $9.81\ h\ (D_2 - D_1)$ N/m²

Where h = Height of circuit

D_1 = Flow density in kg/m³

D_2 = Return density in kg/m³

Note: 9.81 = gravitational unit

(2) Pumped or accelerated system   Where flow of water relies on a pump being incorporated in the return or flowpipe, overcoming the need for large diameter pipes or fittings. Suitable in all conditions whatever distribution pattern is used. i.e. boiler situated on roof.

(3) Basic L.P.H.W. systems

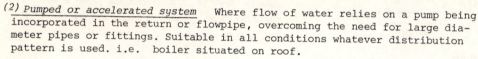

One pipe system

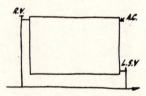

Two pipe system

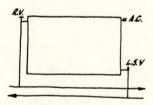

Flow and return water use the same pipe. Water in each successive radiator becoming much cooler.

Each heating element discharges its water into separate return pipe. Pipe sizing smaller — more efficient.

One pipe ring main

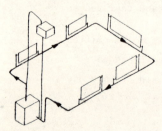

One pipe drop

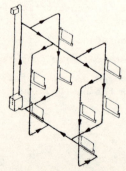

Two pipe riser

One pipe ladder

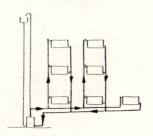 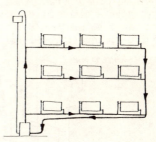

Equalised flow

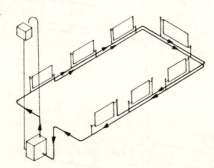

Very efficient system for even distribution of heat. Water in flow and return travel in same direction. Distance of travel of all the water is the same. Flow pipe decreases in size as return pipe increases. More suitable for larger installations.

(3a) *Application of basic systems to high rise buildings*

(Equalised flow, ladder and ring to each floor)

Note: Return pipe taken to top floor before returning to boiler thus giving full equalised flow.

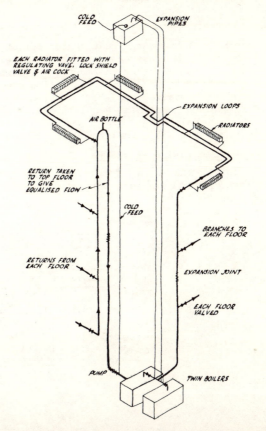

L.P.H.W. SMALL BORE HEATING (12 - 25 mm diam. pipe)

Basic system One pipe or two pipes. Domestic hot water by gravity circulation to indirect cylinder - other circulation system by pump minimum circuit lengths. Smooth bore pipes so minimum friction. Radiators under windows if possible. Pipes lagged under G.F. level. Towel rail on primary circuit.

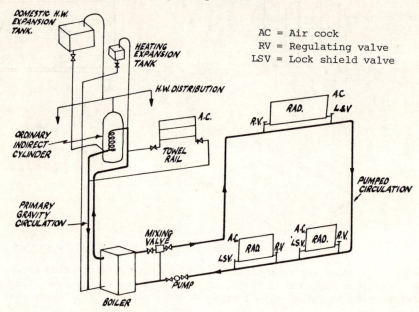

AC = Air cock
RV = Regulating valve
LSV = Lock shield valve

Controls More accurate temp. control so lower running costs

Boiler control	Thermostat - heat source cut at set water temp. 50-80°C.
Central control	Room thermostat - controls pumping time - effective siting needed.
Mixing valve	Manual or by thermostat - allows set amount of return water to by-pass boiler into flow and MIX - suitable for larger installations.
Individual radiator controls	Regulating/Lock shield/Thermostatic radiator/valves.
Time controls	Pre-set automatic on/off system in 24 hour period.

L.P.H.W. MICRO BORE OR MINI BORE SYSTEM

Two pipe principle. Reduced pipe bore 6, 8, 10 mm. Increased water velocities up to 1.8 m/s and each heat emitter with separate flow and return from strategically placed manifold.

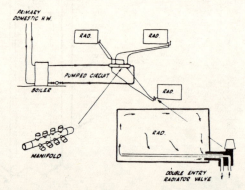

L.P.H.W. HEAT EMITTERS (Radiation and convection in varying degrees)

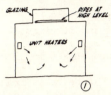

(1) *Exposed piping* Uncommon - e.g. use cloakrooms or high level to pre-heat air under glazing and prevent downdraughts.

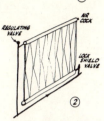

(2) *Radiators* 'Convectors' - Cast Iron (Heavy) Pressed Steel (light Consider support, corrosion and head of water available.

(3) *Skirting heaters* Fin vectors - neat - provides heat skin to external walling. Suitable for higher temp. hot water/ domestic sealed circuit system

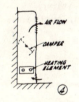

(4) *Convectors* Max. convection, min. radiation. Natural or fan assisted. Independent or continuous, siting below windows and between columns.

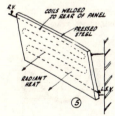

(5) *Radiant panels* Usually high level. Pressed flush steel panel face and pipe coil circulates back to project maximum radiation.

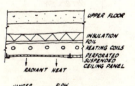

(6) *Ceiling coils* Low temp radiant heat for traditional, heavy, high thermal capacity construction. Modified for suspended ceiling use.

(7) *Unit heaters* Air moved by fan - cold or warm air - quick and adjustable - less pipework frees floor area, reduces floor and ceiling temperature differential.

Generally approx. flow temperature 80-82°C and water to air temperature difference approx. 60°C.

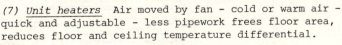
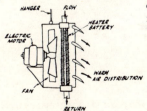

HIGH PRESSURE HOT WATER SYSTEMS

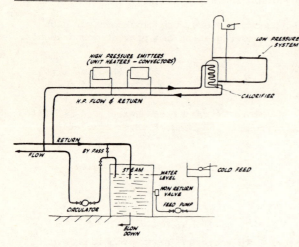

Advantages
(a) *High temperature* (100°C +).
(b) *Smaller pipes* and fittings.
(c) *Long distance mains* possible.
(d) Easier retained high temp *process heating*.
(e) Low pressure can be taken from high pressure by use of *calorifier*.

Pressurisation	By air or nitrogen compressed in enclosed vessel or steam in boiler.
Pumps	In flow header - keeps mains pressure high.
Pipework	Mild steel - butt welded joints - flanged fittings - large radius bends. Easy flow avoids sudden drops in pressure.
Applications	(a) High level radiant heating panels. (b) Strip heating. (c) Unit heaters. (d) Industrial use, cooking, baking, laundries.

MEDIUM PRESSURE - SEALED CIRCUIT DOMESTIC SMALL BORE HEATING

(Water pressurised using membrane pressure vessel with temps approx. 100-110°C.)

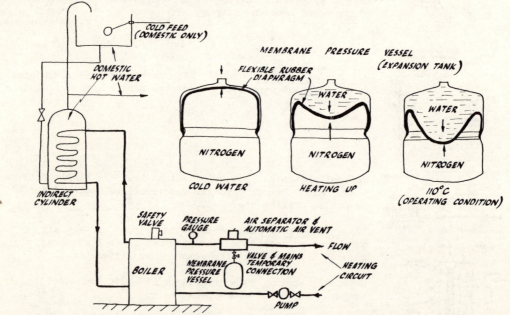

Advantages (a) *Avoids* use of *second* expansion tank. (b) Less oxygen in system *less corrosion*. (c) *No pumping over vent*. (d) *Increased heat emission*.

STEAM HEATING

Not normally used today as a _direct_ means of heating but may be used as the _basic medium_ where steam is being used in industry for process purposes and in hospitals for kitchens, laundry and sterilising. May be passed through calorifiers to produce Low Pressure Hot Water.

Basic principle To obtain from the steam the LATENT heat of condensation from steam to water. (2300 kJ/kg at 100°C)

The temperature of the steam is the same as that of the water from which it has been generated (100°C at atmospheric pressure). Volume of steam approx. 1600 times that of water - hence steam flow pipes much larger than condense return pipes.

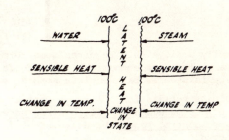

General arrangement of steam unit heaters

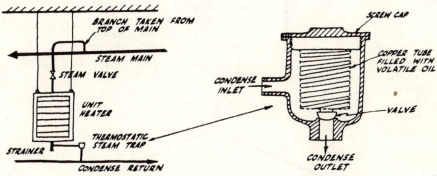

The condense is returned to a collecting tank 'hot well' as quickly as possible - may be pump assisted. Water then pumped to boiler through non-return valve.
Pump controlled by water level regulator attached to side of boiler (float switch at water line).

Steam utilisation for heating

Plenum systems. Central warm air plant with ducting system throughout building.

Unit heaters. Individual steam to warm air 'convectors' - no ducts required. Individual or grouped control of units.

Convectors. As shown with L.P.H.W.

Radiant panels. As shown with L.P.H.W.

Calorifiers. Various types. Tube battery shown Heat transfer to secondary circulation of L.P.H.W.

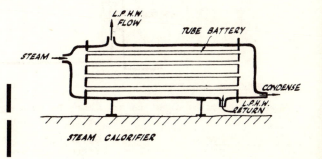

VENTILATION

The causing of air movement. In practice this has become to mean the _regulation_ of air supply to give improved _human comfort_ conditions.

Perfect ventilation depends on

- (a) _Volume_ of air required.
- (b) _Temperature_ of air.
- (c) _Speed_ of movement.
- (d) _Humidity_.
- (e) _Purity_.

To fully achieve this requires some form of _air conditioning system,_ which is very often _not_ economically viable for most buildings. In general the choice is usually between less sophisticated types of ventilation.

(1)NATURAL ventilation   Air _movement_ is brought about in a natural way by the _effect of air temperature differences_ or external air movement (_wind_). _Precise control cannot_ be achieved. Definite _rate of air change cannot_ be achieved.

Forms of natural ventilation.

- (a) Opening sashes in windows.
- (b) Hit and miss ventilators.
- (c) Heating appliance flues.
- (d) Power-less air flow fans.
- (e) Industrial patent roof vents.

Traditional _natural_ cross ventilation may be used to good effect in certain rooms such as classrooms, providing a limited amount of 'control' with varying weather conditions.

   Note: Very little attempt may be made with control of speed, temperature, humidity or purity.

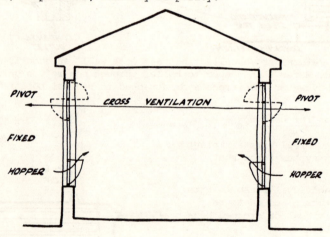

(2)MECHANICAL ventilation

Simple _extract_ or _input_ fans: Controls to a certain degree air movement only. Lacks fine control.

Plenum systems:

(Refer sheet no 39)

Gives better control of air movement - filters air and heats air to required temperature.
Air extraction may or may not be specially provided for.

Air conditioning systems:

(Refer sheet no 40)

Incorporates sophisticated control of air movement, humidity, temperature and purity. May be regarded as essential in certain types of building.

PLENUM SYSTEMS

FILTERED AND WARMED AIR from *central plant* ducted to all parts of the building.

Typical plant situated on roof

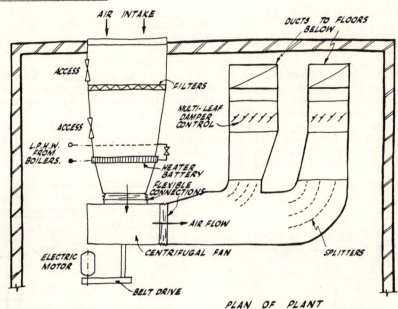

PLAN OF PLANT

SYSTEM COMPRISES

Air intake — Timber louvred - great care in siting - *keep clear* of flues, extractor fans from kitchens and toilets etc. No general solution - *examine possible orientation and sources of contamination*.

Air filtration — Type of filter depends on degree of filtration required - oil coated, expendable or rewashable - roller type fabric filters - electrical precipitation.

Heater — Battery of L.P.H.W., H.P.H.W. or steam heated coils over which air passes and is instantly heated.

Fan — Centrifugal or axial flow type to draw air through intake and discharge, filtered and heated into ducts. Independent electric motor - may be belt driven.

Air ducts — Prefabricated, rectangular galvanised steel, spiral wound, fibreglass or structural type. Avoid sudden restrictions. Multi leaf dampers to control air speeds. Fire dampers used where passing through fire compartment.

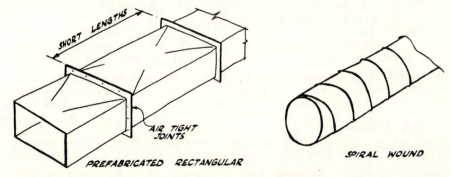

PREFABRICATED RECTANGULAR   SPIRAL WOUND

Grilles — Louvred grilles at termination of ducts into rooms with adjustable louvres (horizontal and vertical) to direct air flow.

AIR CONDITIONING

The *maintaining* of a *desirable internal atmospheric environment* regardless
of external conditions.

Factors involved and which must   (a) Air *temperature*.

be fully controlled: (b) Air *movement*.
    (c) Air *humidity*.
    (d) Air *purity*.
    (e) Radiant solar heat gain.

In Great Britain, air conditioning may be regarded as *desirable* in many types of
building, but may be uneconomical. It may be regarded as *essential* in certain buildings e.g. theatres and cinemas, hospital operating theatres, high precision process
laboratories, computer installations, zoological houses etc.

Note: It is now becoming essential when complete air conditioning is to be installed
that full integrated design takes place with regard to the building envelope,
the process taking place and the building services as a whole – heating,
lighting and ventilation.

There are many *applications* of air condi-   Fundamentally the same basic principles,
tioning, producing a *variety of systems*.   *eliminating* the need of heating by *direct
radiation* and *incorporating* the function of
ventilation.

Basic system using central plant

Suitable where there is one large volume of air (cinemas, halls etc).

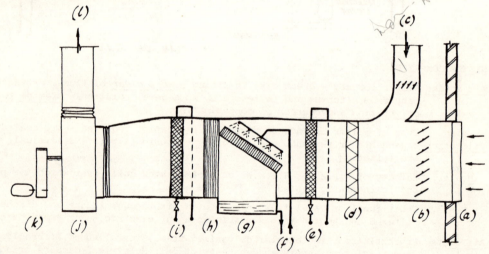

Refer.

(a) Louvred fresh air intake   (g) Air washer (high saturation)
(b) Mixing dampers   (h) Eliminators
(c) Percentage recirculated air   (i) Reheater
(d) Filters   (j) Centrifugal fan
(e) Pre-heater   (k) Motor and belt drive
(f) Water supply   (l) Delivery duct

By control of pre-heater, water temperature and reheater, air may be
chilled below the eventual required temperature at a high humidity and
warmed by reheater, thus raising temperature and lowering relative humidity.

Other types of system

Zoned system.   Building is 'zoned' to cope with differing requirements.
                 Main intake with each zone dealt with by individual plant.

Dual-duct system.   Two ducts (both insulated), one conveying warm air the
                     the other cool air with blenders in each room.

DISTRICT HEATING

Supplying heat to *individual consumer* from *central heat source*.

Energy source

(a) *Direct combustion of fuel* - coal, gas, oil using cheaper fuel grades, transport costs and improved boiler efficiency.

(b) Use of *low grade heat* by-product of electricity generation - (*total energy concept*) (not common in UK).

Insulation

To pipework and buildings *vital* to *conserve energy*.

Heating mediums

(1) Steam (in conjunction with industrial steam process)
(2) H.P.H.W. (flexible and adjustable as to supply and temperature)
(3) L.P.H.W. (suitable for smaller systems).

General arrangement

1. *Heat station* - Consider size, site, access, environmental effect etc.
2. *Distribution* - Radial or ring or interconnection from number of stations. One, two three, or four pipe systems (two popular). N.B. Heat in main so losses in distribution must be minimal.

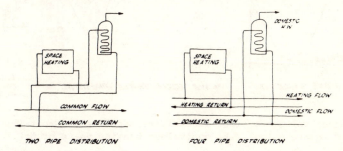

Pipelines

Construction factors. (a) Water table, (b) Sub soil condition
(c) Presence of other pipelines, (d) Economics.

E.g. types (a) Single conduit with gas conc. surround. (b) Double conduit.
(c) Open trench with insulation.

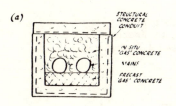 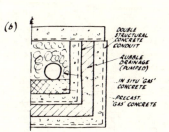 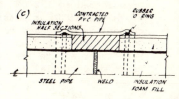

(Joint detail)

Economics may dictate the use of high level pipelines.

Consumer installations

Basically conventional space heating systems with calorifier links to separate buildings (steam HP to Water LP).

For more complete details of Heating and Ventilating refer I.H.V.E. Guide.

ELECTRICAL INSTALLATIONS
INTRODUCTION

FUNDAMENTALS

Quantity	Unit	Symbol	Analogy with water
Electric current	ampere	A	Rate of flow
Electric potential	volt	V	Pressure
Resistance	ohm	Ω	Frictional resistance
Power	watt	W	Working rate
$W = V \times A$	$V = A \times R$	$W = A^2 \times R$	$A = V/R$

Type of current   (a) <u>Direct</u> (dc) Flows in one direction only
                   (b) <u>Alternating</u> (ac) Represented by sine wave shown (50 Hz)

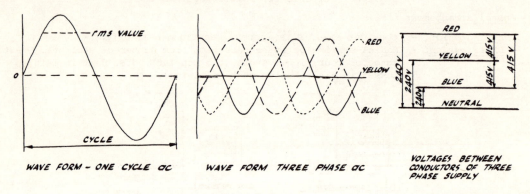

WAVE FORM - ONE CYCLE *ac*   WAVE FORM THREE PHASE *ac*   VOLTAGES BETWEEN CONDUCTORS OF THREE PHASE SUPPLY

The nominal (phase) voltage of most electricity supplies in Great Britain is *240 volts* (rms = root mean square value) (The equivalent heating value of dc).

Power supply organisation. Central Electricity Generating Board (C.E.G.B.)
                               Steam, hydro, diesel and nuclear power (Some private plant)

<u>The Grid System</u>. Vast overhead and underground cable system linked together providing
                    pool of electricity supply.

General distribution

50 Hz alternating current generators: 11 000-33 000 V.
Transformed to 132 000 V to carry over long distances to sub stations (could be 275 000, 400 000, or possibly 750 000 V). $W = V \times A$ therefore by *increasing* voltage current is *decreased* to give the same power - cable decreased in size.
Sub station step down transformer to 11 000 V.
Factory or estate transformer 11 000 to 415/240 V.
Ratio of potential 415 to 240 = 1.732 or $\sqrt{3}$.

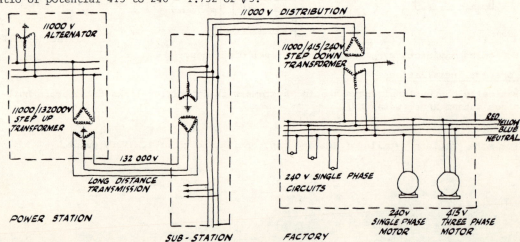

POWER STATION   SUB-STATION   FACTORY

BASIC ELECTRICAL REGULATIONS

(a) *Electricity (Factories Act)* (1944)
(b) *Electricity Supply Regulations* (1937) } Legally enforceable
(c) Institution of Electrical Engineers –
 Regulations for the Electrical Equipment
 of Buildings (1970)
 (Date back to 1882 – constantly being
 amended – Fourteenth edition 1966)

NOT legally binding but
accepted as efficient
standards by Boards, Contractors
and Industrial & Domestic
consumers.

Note: I.E.E. Regs. cover Installation, Inspection, Testing and Maintenance.
 Embody main requirements to ensure safety – freedom from fire and shock.

Basic installation principles

Voltages. (a) Extra low Not exceeding 30 V
 (b) Low   Exceeding 30 V N.E. 250 V
 (c) Medium   Exceeding 250 V N.E. 650 V
 (d) High   Exceeding 650 V

Service cable. Property of electricity authority up to meter position.
 Extensive variation in actual cost.

Isolation. Required in the event of accident or during servicing.

Cable. Conductor – material of low resistance to current flow (copper,aluminium)
 Insulant – material of high resistance to current flow (p.v.c. paper)

Cable rating. All cables assigned rating in the I.E.E. Regs. Adequate to take current
 to avoid overheating and to take voltage drop which must not exceed 2.5 %
 See I.E.E.Reg. tables M1 to M33.

Protect against: excess current   electric shock

            Fuses   Earthing

          Rewirable   Connection of all metallic parts
          Cartridge   to earth with low resistance
        Circuit breaker   giving heavy current flow, blowing
                             fuse and making system safe.

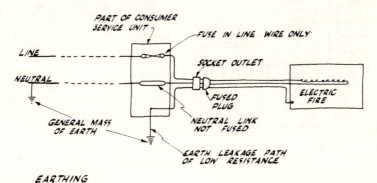

EARTHING

Earthing to outer metallic sheath of service cable or earth plate.
Note. Water pipes *not* now regarded as satisfactory due to possible
 replacement by plastic or asbestos pipes at later date.

MAIN INTAKE AND EQUIPMENT (DOMESTIC)

Consumer Service Control Unit

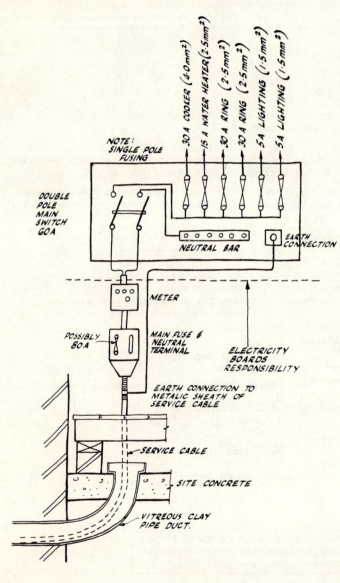

30 A COOKER (4·0 mm²)

15 A WATER HEATER (2·5 mm²)

30 A RING (2·5 mm²)

30 A RING (2·5 mm²)

5 A LIGHTING (1·5 mm²)

5 A LIGHTING (1·5 mm²)

NOTE:
SINGLE POLE
FUSING

DOUBLE
POLE
MAIN
SWITCH
60 A

NEUTRAL BAR

EARTH
CONNECTION

METER

POSSIBLY
80 A

MAIN FUSE &
NEUTRAL
TERMINAL

ELECTRICITY
BOARDS
RESPONSIBILITY

EARTH CONNECTION TO
METALIC SHEATH OF
SERVICE CABLE

SERVICE CABLE

SITE CONCRETE

VITREOUS CLAY
PIPE DUCT.

Note

Electricity Board's *main fuse* possibly 80 A – this is a variable.

Electricity Board's *service cable* may be of the concentric type with neutral outer conductor being earthed.

Double pole main switch – trend is for 80 or 100 A.

Final ring sub circuits one or two may be used.

Cooker fuse – trend to increase to 45 or 60 A.

LIGHTING CIRCUITS

Loop in method

Live and neutral looped in and out of each
ceiling rose. Switch, single pole, in live
wire.Earth wire used linking ceiling roses
and switch.

Switching Two way used to control group of
lighting outlets from two positions.

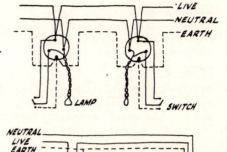

POWER CIRCUITS

Domestic ring final sub-circuit

Universally employed. Twin core cable (2.5 mm²)
with earth. Live wire from 30 A fuseway to
each socket outlet in turn and back to fuseway. Neutral starts and finishes at neutral
bar. Earth starts and finishes at earth
terminal.

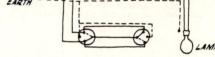

13 A socket outlets and square pin fused plugs. Based on largest appliance - 3 kW fire.

$$W = V \times A$$
$$= 240 \times 13$$
$$= \underline{3120 \text{ watts}}$$

3 A and 13 A fuses recommended for use

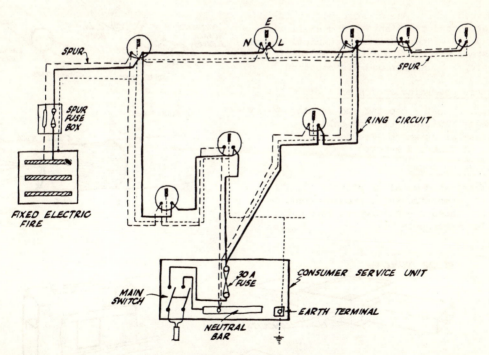

Domestic ring final sub-circuit may serve an unlimited number of socket outlets but
shall not serve a floor area of more than 100 m². Often TWO ring circuits used to one
property with socket outlets evenly distributed between the two.
Spurs.Not more than two socket outlets or one fixed appliance fitted to any one spur.
Total number of spurs shall not exceed the total number of socket outlets and
stationary appliances connected directly to the ring.

Important that number and relative position of socket outlets should be given careful consideration. Socket outlets generally, are _not_ for the use of a _specific_
appliance but for the convenience of using almost any appliance in any position.

46

WIRING SYSTEMS

In general, systems may be *exposed* or *concealed* depending upon *degree of security*. This may influence screed thicknesses and size of chases etc. Cable runs horizontal and vertical - easier location - reducing accidental damage.

TYPES OF SYSTEM

(a) All insulated sheathed wiring. Conductors individually insulated - p.v.c.,t.r.s. and p.c.p. with outer mechanical protective sheath of the same material.

(b) Conduit system. Metal or plastic tubing into which cables are *drawn*. Surface mounted or concealed by plaster. System protects cables from mechanical damage, minimises fire risk, provides means of easy rewiring.

(c) Mineral insulated cable systems (MICC,MICS) Single strand conductors of copper or aluminium with thin tube of same metal with space between packed with magnesium oxide.

(d) Armoured cable. One or more p.v.c. insulated conductors sheathed overall with p.v.c and protected from mechanical damage by steel wire with a further protection of p.v.c. - underground distribution.

Factors governing choice of system

Relative cost - capital and maintenance. Ease of rewiring. Life of cable. Mechanical strength. Freedom from risk of fire and shock.

TRUNKING SYSTEMS

Prefabricated metal or plastic - may be compartmented . provide continuous access - used where cables follow same route.

(a) All insulated

(b) Conduit

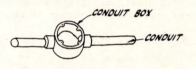

(c) M.I.C.C.

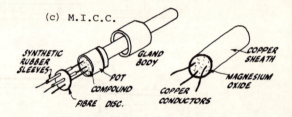

(d) Armoured

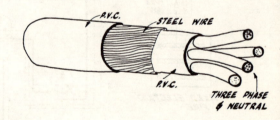

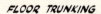

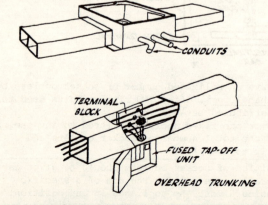

FLOOR TRUNKING

OVERHEAD TRUNKING

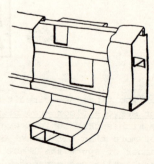

SKIRTING & UNDERFLOOR TRUNKING

BUSBARS

Uninsulated bars copper or aluminium 10-20 mm diam. or up to 40 x 100 mm flats. Used where current exceeds 100 A per phase. Enables tap-offs to be re-arranged conveniently.

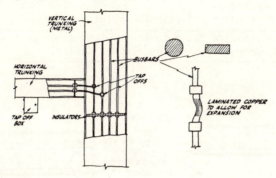

LARGE SCALE DISTRIBUTION

System into sections like large scale domestic consumer service unit.

1. *Radial distribution* - Group of buildings fed via individual lines from one intake - bus bar chamber connection main switch to fused switches.

2. *Ring distribution* -Site ringed by heavy cable - enables separate isolation of sections yet maintaining rest of installation.

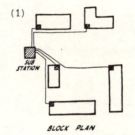

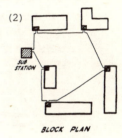

3. *Rising main* distribution - Used for *high rise development*. Arranged with:

Vertical busbar to distribution boards on separate floors, or alternate floors with simple loop circuit to separate flat consumer units.

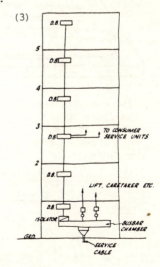

Note: Transformer chambers if load in excess of 100 kW . Electricity board may require supply in at 11 kV and transformed to 415/240 V with'feed out rights'.

HEATING *Electric floor warming systems*. Refer: CP 1018:1971.

Low temperature *radiant* heat. Warm feet - cool head - desirable conditions. Lower air temperature will suffice where radiant temperature greater, therefore less heat loss through walls and ceilings.
Excessive air movement eliminated and pattern staining reduced.

Principles: Screed and/or concrete floor together with structure has thermal storage capacity. Heat supplied during the night at cheaper tariff.

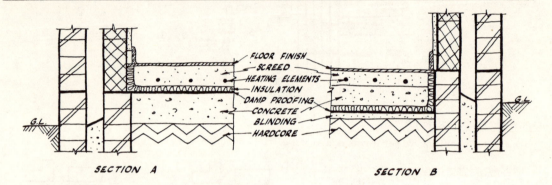

SECTION A   SECTION B

Types of system.

(a) Ducted   (b) Embedded

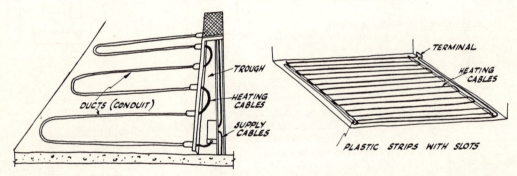

Heating elements *passed through conduits* within floor screed. Easily withdrawn in case of fault. Requires trough down one or both sides of room. *Used for expensive floor finishes.*

Heating elements *bedded solid* in floor screed. Terminal boxes from each panel Saving in capital cost but maintenance could be greater.

Factors governing thermal capacity.

(a) Thickness of screed. 50 to 75 mm depending on hours of off peak electricity supply.
(b) Insulation.   Min. 25 mm to approx. 50 mm depending on dryness of site.
                         Mineral wool, expanded polystyrene, cork. Whole floor may be
                         insulated if carpeted or outer metre perimeter only if un-
                         carpeted.
(c) Element. Should *not* be laid direct on insulation - possible overheating.
             Should not be pushed into contact with itself - possible overheating.
             Should be monitored during screeding - detection of damage.
    Screed. Should be cured and gradually brought up to full load.
Approx. Loading. 150 W/m² .

REFER ALSO TO HEATING AND VENTILATION SHEETS NO. 26 - 31

TEMPORARY AND CONSTRUCTION SITE INSTALLATIONS

Ref. CP 1017:1969 and BS 4363.

Regulations	In general as for permanent installations except that regulation regarding cable supports may be relaxed. *In addition* installation should be in charge of competent person accepting full responsibility for safety (name and designation of such person prominently displayed). Installation *tested* at intervals of 3 months or less. Installation subject to requirements of the 'Electricity (Factories Act) Special Regulations'.

Notification: Given to Supply Authority at early planning stage.

Points to be discussed with the Supply Authority

       (a) Can temporary supply position be the same as permanent position?
       (b) Is high voltage supply necessary?
       (c) Metering and tariff arrangements.
       (d) Anticipated connection date.
       (e) Supply system detail.
       (f) Provision of earth.
       (g) Location of main distribution point.
       (h) Precautions to be taken with existing service lines.

Equipment used should embody the following factors

       (a) Flexibility in application for repeated use.
       (b) Suitable to transport and store.
       (c) Robust in construction to resist damage.
       (d) Safety in use.

Distribution voltages

Mains voltage   1. Three-phase 415 V 4-wire
                  2. Single-phase 240 V

Reduced   1. 110 V three-phase
   voltage   2. 110 V single-phase
                  3. 50 V single-phase
                  4. 25 V single-phase

Application recommendations

1. Fixed plant	415 V 3-phase
2. Movable plant fed by trailing cable	415 V 3-phase
3. Installations in site buildings	240 V 1-phase
4. Fixed flood lighting	240 V 1-phase
5. Portable and hand held tools	110 V 3 or 1-phase
6. Site lighting other than flood lighting	110 V 1-phase
7. Portable hand lamps (general)	110 V 1-phase
8. Portable hand lamps (confined and damp situations)	50 or 25 V 1-phase

Earthing.   Main earth connection generally supplied by the Supply Authority.

Colour coding for plugs and socket outlets

25 V	Violet	110 V	Yellow	415 V	Red
50 V	White	240 V	Blue	650 V	Black

Cabling.   For *site offices* etc. - all as I.E.E. Regs.
                 For *all other parts of installation* - cables carrying 415/240 V should be protected and their *route marked*.

Typical arrangement of distribution units, etc.

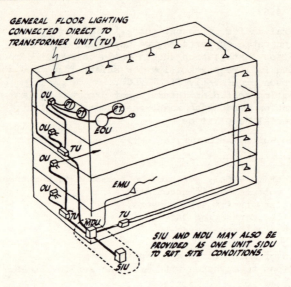

GENERAL FLOOR LIGHTING
CONNECTED DIRECT TO
TRANSFORMER UNIT (TU)

SIU AND MDU MAY ALSO BE
PROVIDED AS ONE UNIT SIDU
TO SUIT SITE CONDITIONS.

BS CODE OF PRACTICE 1017

(SIU)	Supply incoming unit.
(SIDU)	Supply incoming and distribution unit.
(MDU)	Main distribution unit.
(TU/1)	Transformer unit, single phase only.
(TU/3)	Transformer unit, three phase only.
(TU/1/3)	Transformer unit, single and three phase.
(OU)	Outlet unit - an assembly of equipment providing facilities for the control, protection, and connection of final sub circuits operating at 110 V fed by a 32 A supply.

    (OU/1) Four double-pole socket outlets (single phase)
    (OU/3) Two three-pole socket outlets.

(EOU)	Extension outlet unit.
(EMU)	Earth monitor unit.
(PT)	Portable tool up to 1.5 kW.
($\triangle$)	Lighting.

Refer   I.E.E.Regulations
            Code of Practice 1017:1969
            Building Research Establishment Digests
            D. of E. Advisory leaflets

LIFTS   Installation and design is highly specialised work, involving a number of patents.
Power. Electric - greater speeds - automatic control.
May be hydraulic or hand operated.
Types; Passenger - Hospital - Goods - Service.

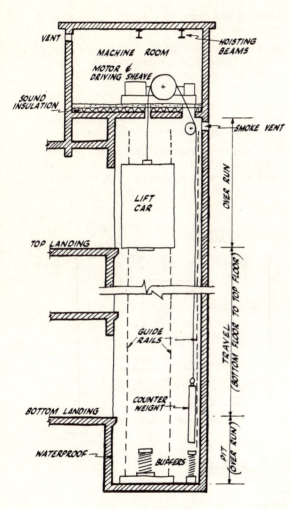

Machine room

Normally placed above shaft - cheaper and more satisfactory. Alternative siting requires greater rope lengths and diverter sheaves. *Sound insulation* required against vibrations and sharp penetrating noise of clicking of electrical contacts.
Natural or mechanical *ventilation*.
Power socket outlets for wandering leads.

Lift well

Smooth face - Plumb - within manufacturers tolerances. Set out from fixed datum.
Ventilated for smoke escape.
No other services in well or machine room.

Over-run and pit

Amount of over-run depends on lift speed.
Pit fitted with spring loaded or oil loaded buffers - depends on lift speed.

Car

'Sling' formed of steel angles and channels.
Finish largely depends on type of building.
Good ventilation and artificial lighting.
Access hatch - cuts off electricity supply when opened.
Safety cams fitted to car, tighten on guides if power fails.
Alarm system - contact with ground floor entrance or caretaker's flat etc.

Lifting machinery

Car balanced by counterbalance weights.
3 phase a.c. supply may be used for slow lifts. Variable voltage d.c. used for higher speed lifts giving smoother running, rapid acceleration, more accurate floor levelling, quieter, less overheating and less servicing required.

Factors to be considered in estimating number of lifts required

(a) Type of building - offices, flats, hotels etc.
(b) Population to be transported in given time.
(c) System of control and floor stops.
(d) Capacity of individual lifts.
(e) Speed of lift.
(f) Maximum allowable waiting time.

Refer   CP 407:1972
        BS 2655
        Building Regs. Sect E10 (8)
        Examination - Factories
        Acts 1937, Sect 22
        Fire and Local Authority
        Requirements

PATERNOSTERS

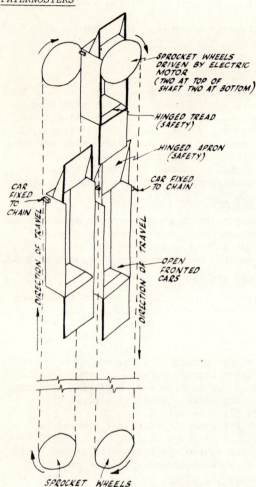

SPROCKET WHEELS DRIVEN BY ELECTRIC MOTOR (TWO AT TOP OF SHAFT TWO AT BOTTOM)

HINGED TREAD (SAFETY)

HINGED APRON (SAFETY)

CAR FIXED TO CHAIN

CAR FIXED TO CHAIN

DIRECTION OF TRAVEL

DIRECTION OF TRAVEL

OPEN FRONTED CARS

SPROCKET WHEELS

Continuous moving, open fronted cars attached at opposite diagónal corners at top of car to two endless chains driven by sprocket wheels. (Two cars for each floor plus two).
Landing and car floor nosings are hinged to prevent injury.

Particularly suited to medium and high rise buildings where there is a large proportion of *internal movement* of occupants.

Speed approx 1/3 m/s. Lift usually provided alongside paternoster for use of handicapped persons, goods etc.

Very reliable and require comparatively little maintenance due to steady contin- uous running as compared with the lift.

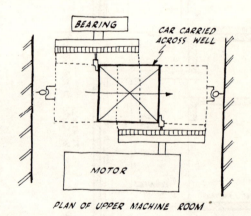

BEARING

CAR CARRIED ACROSS WELL

MOTOR

PLAN OF UPPER MACHINE ROOM

ESCALATORS

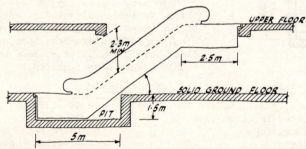

UPPER FLOOR

2·3m MIN

2·5m

SOLID GROUND FLOOR

1·5m

PIT

5m

Installed where there is usually a continuous flow of passengers (department stores etc). May be grouped in different ways to give variations of two way flow. *Speed* normally ½ m/s. Width of stair approx 2/3 - 1 metre requiring 1½ - 2 m width of opening respectively.

Problems requiring careful consideration

Fire spread. Possibly enclosed in separate fire compartment or use of automatic shutters.
Delivered as a unit. *Adequate access required.*

WITHDRAWN

NATURAL

Advantages.   Gives better *three-dimensional quality* when side lighting.
Provides an *external awareness* - still very important to most people.
A level of approx. *500 lux* at ground level from an *overcast sky* in
this country.

Disadvantages.   Variable in both quantity and quality - sky glare. Depth of
penetration and therefore building limited. High unit heat loss
through glass.
Condensation problems increased.
Solar heat gain problems increased.
Sound problems increased.

> In daylighting design in Great Britain the *overcast sky* is taken as being the
> critical daylighting conditions.

Definition of units

Daylight factor.

The illumination at a specified internal point expressed as a percentage of the
simultaneous horizontal illumination outdoors (No direct sunlight) Unit - %

Sky factor.

The illumination at a specified internal point that would have been received directly
through an *unglazed* opening from a sky of *uniform luminance* expressed as a percentage
of the horizontal illumination under an unobstructed hemisphere of the same sky. Unit - %
or ratio.

Sky component.

The illumination reaching a specified internal point directly from the sky, expressed
as a percentage of the simultaneous horizontal illumination outdoors. Unit - %

Externally reflected component.

The illumination reaching a specified internal point directly from exterior reflecting
surfaces expressed as a percentage of the simultaneous horizontal illumination outdoors.
Unit - %

Internal reflected component.

The illumination reaching a specified internal point directly from internal reflecting
surfaces expressed as a percentage of the simultaneous horizontal illumination outdoors.
Unit - %

Maintenance factor.

The ratio of the illumination or daylight factor expected in normal operation to
that prevailing under perfectly clean conditions. Unit - dimensionless ratio.

> Daylight factor comprising - Sky component + External reflected component +
> Internal reflected component

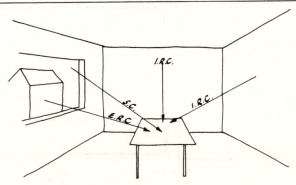

To calculate daylight factor.

Add the three separately calculated components. *Corrections* for glazing materials, dirt, window frames etc. can be applied to the total daylight factor

Factors calculated by use of B.R.E. daylight protractors (set of ten protractors).

Practical determination of daylight factor. Use of daylight factor meter.

Meter is calibrated directly as daylight factor percentages working in same manner as a light meter.

Recommended daylight factors. (Extracts from I.E.S. Code of Practice.)

Building	Space	D.F. % not less than
Offices	General	2
	Typing	4
	Drawing boards	6
Assembly halls	Foyers	1
	Corridors	0.5
	Stairs	1
Domestic	Kitchens	2
	Living rooms	1
	Bedrooms	0.5
Schools	Classrooms	2

Daylight Area

The daylight area related to a given daylight factor may be presented as the area enclosed by a contour line drawn through all points on the working plane on which the daylight factor is of that given value.

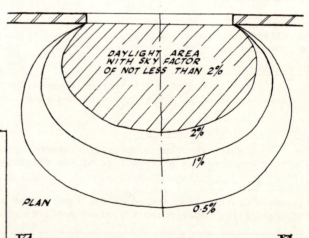

PLAN

DAYLIGHT AREA WITH SKY FACTOR OF NOT LESS THAN 2%

2%

1%

0.5%

It is recommended that the re-commended daylight factors should cover a set daylight area for a certain percentage of the floor area (variable with type of building).
This may entail increasing the size of the window area or re-positioning windows or introducing *artificial lighting* to certain areas of the room.

Vertical section showing daylight distribution (taken on centre line - working plane).

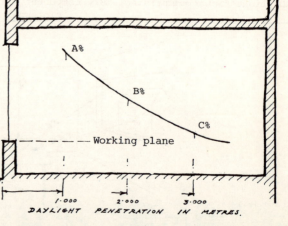

A%

B%

C%

Working plane

1·000   2·000   3·000

DAYLIGHT PENETRATION IN METRES.

ARTIFICIAL

Standards of electric lighting today can be very high and there are many buildings where this may be the only type of lighting used.

Advantages. Better control - constant - not considerable heat gain - building depth not limited - solar heat gain problems may be minimised - sky glare minimised - noise problems minimised.

The modern trend is generally for *less natural lighting* and more artificial lighting with the environmental advantages this brings.

Design criteria

Quantity. Amount of light falling on working plane. Illumination levels given in the Illuminating Engineering Society's Code.

Some typical values

Room	Illumination level	Limiting glare index
Offices (general)	500 (lux)	19
Conference rooms	750	16
Drawing boards	750	16
Classrooms	500	19
Watchmaking (minute processes)	3000	19
Living rooms (general)	50	–
Living rooms (casual reading)	150	–
Kitchens	300	–

(Old people's homes) Illuminances should be increased by 50 to 100% - avoid glare as much as possible.

Quality. As shown, a limiting glare index is given in code.
Glare -(discomfort or disability glare)- both caused by degree of brightness and direction of light source.

Light emitted within 35° of vertical will not cause serious glare. This is catered for by using *suitable lighting fittings.* These are categorised BZ1 to BZ10. (British zonal method of classification depending on direction of light output).

General types of lamp.
(a) General lighting service lamp.
(b) Reflector lamp.
(c) Fluorescent tube.

Factors governing choice. Capital cost - running costs - lamp life - possible vibrations - type of colour.

TUNGSTEN

DISPERSIVE INDUSTRIAL REFLECTOR

SPHERICAL DIFFUSER OPEN BENEATH

OPAL SPHERE

OPEN TOP DIFFUSER.

FLUORESCENT

*BATTEN
LUMINAIRE*

PLASTIC TROUGH.

*ENCLOSED
PLASTIC
DIFFUSER*

*CEILING MOUNTED
LOUVRE PANEL*

Heat gain. When lighting level is above 500 lux, then heat from lamps may have to be dealt with, either by extracting and exhausting or used in a heat recovery integrated design system to help heat the building.

Simple design for an average illuminance

Terminology.

Unit	Term	Definition
Luminous intensity	Candela (cd)	Intensity of light at its source
Luminous flux	Lumen (lm)	Measure of flow of light emitted by 1 candela
Illumination	Lux (lx)	Light falling on unit area (per square metre)

Lumen method.

Basic formula $$N = \frac{A \times E}{F \times UF \times MF}$$

where N = Number of lighting fittings
A = Area at working plane height (m²)
E = Illumination level required (lux)
F = 'Average through life' lamp flux (lumens)
UF = Utilisation factor
MF = Maintenance factor

Utilisation factor. A measure of the degree to which the potential of the installed lamp has been usefully applied. Takes into account - shape of room (room index) - reflection factors and performance of lighting fitting (obtained from manufacturer's tables).

Maintenance factor. An allowance for the lamp not being perfectly clean. e.g. if only 80% of the light is getting through, then MF of 0.8 must be taken to allow for this.

Example. Determine the number of 4 300 lm fittings required to produce an illumination of 400 lux on the working plane of an office 15 m x 9 m x 3 m high (working plane 1 m above floor level)   UF = 0.56, MF = 0.8.

$$N = \frac{A \times E}{F \times UF \times MF}$$

$$= \frac{(15 \times 9) \times 400}{4300 \times 0.56 \times 0.8}$$

$$= \underline{28.03} \text{ (say 28 fittings)}$$

Spacing of fittings must not exceed 1½ times mounting height above working plane. (1¼ times in case of louvred or recessed fittings).

In this example 1½ x 2 = maximum spacing of 3 metres.

Actual spacing. Could be 9/4 m = 2.250 and 15/7 = 2.143 m.

> *Note: Complete uniformity of illumination is not possible, but if the minimum illumination is at least 70% of the maximum then this may be regarded as uniform.*

GAS SERVICES

Supply.   Gradual changeover in recent years from TOWN GAS to NATURAL GAS.
           Town gas eventually *phased out* altogether.

Characteristics

Town gas.   Of different manufactured fuel gases varying in composition.
             Hydrogen content approx. 50 %. Calorific value 18.62 MJ/m³.

Natural   No hydrogen. Approx. 94 % methane. Calorific value 37.26 MJ/m³.
gas.   Higher pressure - smaller pipe sizes or increased capacity.

Safety.   When ignited in a confined space, gas/air mixtures will explode regardless
           of volume. *Leaks of any type are extremely dangerous*. Gas undertakings em-
           powered to refuse connection if appliances are below standard.
           Confederation of Registered Gas Installers (CORGI) set up to improve
           standards.

Mains.   Area Gas Board responsible up to and including meters. *Pressures vary*
          and reduce from initial main to branch domestic mains. May be *boosted* on
          consumer's premises for *industry*.

Domestic installations

Note: Gas installations should not start on site before agreement with area board.

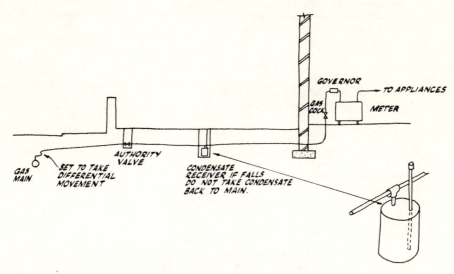

Service pipe should rise slightly from main (1 in 12) or condensate receiver may
be required at lower point to enable removal of condensate.

Control provided by 90° lever operated *gas cock* then gas service *governor* and *meter*.

Meter by-pass only provided in larger installations where continuity of supply is
vital to enable meter to be replaced without interruption to supply (industry).

Pipe sizing depends on gas pressure and friction set up by length of pipe and number
of bends and fittings etc. Generous allowances usually made to cater for future
increases in number of appliances.

GAS INSTALLATION (B)

Builder's work

Valve and condensation pits. Small inspection chambers - brick with metal covers.

Pipe sleeves. These should be provided where pipes pass through walls etc. guards
against settlement. Avoids cutting and making good.
Forms stop for gas leaks into cavity.

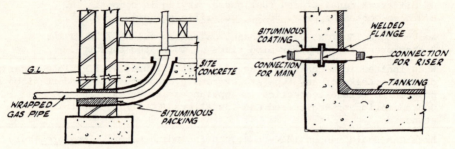

GAS INTAKES TO BUILDING

Building in pipes. Wrap with protection tape if passing through plaster (anti-
corrosion.
Generous screed thicknesses required.
Avoid gas pipes passing through sealed cavities - ventilate
and form pipe in *one* length.

Gas flues

Purpose.

    (i) To remove products of combustion
   (ii) To assist in room ventilation.

To reduce flue condensation.

    (i) Install flue *inside building*.
   (ii) Keep flue *short*.
  (iii) *Insulate* flue
   (iv) Install *flue linings*
    (v) Use *double walled* flue pipe

Some possible advantage trends with Natural Gas

    (a) Competitive tariffs for large quantities.
    (b) Enables wider use of 'total energy' systems (industry).
    (c) Ideal fuel for roof top boiler plant.
    (d) Increased pressure - higher calorific value - smaller pipes.
    (e) Suitable for large scale refrigeration and air conditioning.

FIREFIGHTING EQUIPMENT AND PROTECTION SYSTEMS

Legislation

The Building Regulations
The Building Standards (Scotland)
London Building Acts
Public Health Act
Factories Act
Offices Shops and Railway Premises Act
School Premises Regulations
Cinematograph (Safety) Regulations
Theatres Act
Licensing Act
The Gaming Act
Electricity Supply Regulations
The Fire Precautions Act

Note: Local building acts and bye-laws should be consulted

Types of equipment
(a) *Portable*
(b) Fixed (*First Aid*)
(c) Fixed (*Fire Brigade use*)
(d) Fixed (*Sprinklers, Drenchers* etc)

(a) Portable
(i) Water buckets (9 litres)
(ii) Sand buckets (use on electrical apparatus)
(iii) Soda/acid (bicarbonate of soda dissolved in water with separate phial of sulphuric acid - carbon dioxide generated when mixed). Water acts as extinguisher - gas provides power to jet. (10 litres capacity for 250 m² floor area).
(iv) Foam extinguishers - mixing of chemicals generating gas pressure and foam - extinguishes fire by the exclusion of oxygen - suitable for burning liquids.
(v) Carbon dioxide - compressed or stored as liquid. Does not cause damage to materials.
(vi) Asbestos or glass fibre blankets to wrap around people - domestic and workshop and laboratory use.

(b) Fixed (First Aid)
Metal hose reels and rubber hose connected to water supply. (Delivery requirement 0.4 litres/s at distance of 6 m from nozzle). 21 m static head required - minimum pipe connections 50 mm.
May be supplied direct from main or tanked.
May require pumping to high rise buildings.

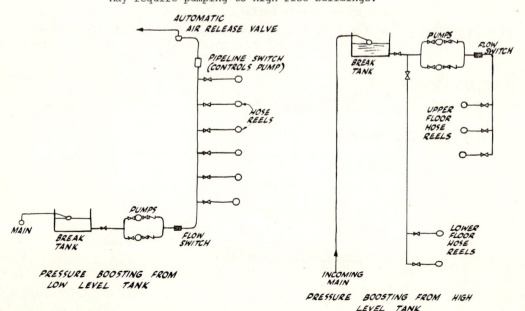

PRESSURE BOOSTING FROM LOW LEVEL TANK

PRESSURE BOOSTING FROM HIGH LEVEL TANK

Acknowledgement to I.H.V.E. Guide Book B for sketches reproduction.

(c) **Fixed**
(Fire Brigade use)

(i) <u>External hydrants</u> Generally not necessary if adequate public supply exists within 90 m of building. Used for large industrial complexes, hospitals etc.

(Refer IHVE Guide for more complete details as may be required)

(ii) <u>Internal hydrants</u>
Dry risers.Buildings 18-60 m high. Charged by fire brigade as required. Inlets on external wall within 18 m of access road.
Wet risers.Buildings over 60 m high. Normally 100 mm diam. Pressure not less than 410 kN/m² - permanently connected to water supply. Each hydrant valve padlocked in closed position. May be phased into commission as construction proceeds.

(iii) <u>Foam installations</u> 75 mm dia pipe leading from outside building to boiler rooms and oil storage chambers etc.

(d) <u>Fixed</u>

(i) <u>Sprinklers</u>. - Automatic - do *not* require occupancy of building for operation. *Advantageous for buildings of high fire risk -* may be statutory requirement under local legislation.Water held back by quartzoid bulb. Temperature rise breaks bulb at 68-180°C (or special higher). Flow of water operates fire alarm.

Water supply: (a) Public mains
(b) Elevated private reservoir
(c) Automatic pump
(d) Pressure tank
(e) Elevated tanks

Type of system: (a) Wet pipe
(b) Dry pipe
(c) Alternate (summer/winter)

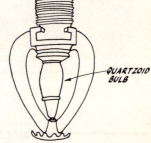

QUARTZOID BULB

TYPICAL SPRINKLER HEAD

(ii) <u>Drencher</u>. - Discharge of water over *external openings* of building to prevent spread of fire from or to adjacent premises. System of pipework with drencher discharge nozzles at intervals (e.g. above proscenium arch of theatre at stage side for protection of safety curtain).

(e) <u>Carbon dioxide.</u> Suitable for use on fires involving flammable liquids and electrical risks - transformer chambers and switchgear rooms. Room flooded with gas to approx. 50 % volume of room.

Other installations

Dry chemical
Vapourising liquid

Fire detection (automatic)

Enables early warning and so earlier attack on fire. May detect

(a) Smoke
(b) Heat
(c) Flame

These systems can be used *independently* or *combined*. Useful in *buildings of high fire risk* which may be *unoccupied for long periods*.